INDIGO

CREDITS

DESIGNS & STYLING
Kim Hargreaves

EDITOR
Kathleen Hargreaves

PHOTOGRAPHY & EDITORIAL DESIGN
Graham Watts

MODEL
Fiona Beck

HAIR & MAKE-UP
Diana Fisher

LAYOUTS
Angela Lin

PATTERNS
Sue Whiting & Trisha McKenzie

© Copyright Kim Hargreaves 2012
First published in 2012 by Kim Hargreaves, Intake Cottage, 26 Underbank Old Road, Holmfirth, West Yorkshire, HD9 1EA, England.

British Library Cataloguing in Publication Data
A catalogue record for this book is available from the British Library

ISBN-10   1-906487-13-3
ISBN-13   978-1-906487-13-3

CONTENTS

INTO THE
BLUE...

S ubtle textures and sleek contours
mixed with a dash of low-key chic
sums-up the season's understated look,
whilst an array of deliciously vibrant
shades hold the key to making these
effortless pieces zing.

AZURE // LONG-LINE BOYFRIEND CARDIGAN

SAND // WIDE TEXTURED SWEATER

CERULEAN // VOLUMINOUS SLOUCHY SWEATER

OUT OF THE BLUE...

ENTICE

Close-fitting cardigan with sweetheart neckline

Recommendation

Suitable for the knitter with a little experience
Please see pages 10 & 11 for photographs.

	XS	S	M	L	XL	XXL	
To fit	**81**	**86**	**91**	**97**	**102**	**109**	**cm**
bust	32	34	36	38	40	43	in

Rowan Siena 4 ply

	9	10	11	11	12	12	x 50gm

Photographed in Vindaloo

Needles

1 pair 2mm (no 14) (US 0) needles
1 pair 2¾mm (no 12) (US 2) needles
2.50mm (no 12) (US C2) crochet hook

Buttons – 13

Tension

28 sts and 42 rows to 10 cm measured over
pattern using 2¾mm (US 2) needles.

Crochet abbreviations

ch = chain; **dc** = double crochet; **ss** = slip
stitch; **tr** = treble.
See page 99 for further details.

BACK

Cast on 108 (114: 122: 128: 136: 146) sts
using 2mm (US 0) needles.
Beg and ending rows as indicated, working
chart rows 1 to 10 **once only** and then
repeating chart rows 11 to 22 **throughout**,
cont in patt from chart as folls:
Work 10 rows, ending with a WS row.
Change to 2¾mm (US 2) needles.
Keeping patt correct, dec 1 st at each end of
15th and 2 foll 8th rows, then on 4 foll 6th
rows. 94 (100: 108: 114: 122: 132) sts.
Cont straight until back measures 21 (21: 22:
22: 22: 22) cm, ending with a WS row.
Inc 1 st at each end of next and 3 foll 10th
rows, then on 3 foll 12th rows, taking inc sts
into patt. 108 (114: 122: 128: 136: 146) sts.
Work 13 rows, ending with a WS row.

Shape armholes

Keeping patt correct, cast off 4 (4: 5: 5: 6: 6)
sts at beg of next 2 rows.
100 (106: 112: 118: 124: 134) sts.
Dec 1 st at each end of next 3 (5: 5: 7: 7: 9)
rows, then on foll 2 (2: 4: 3: 5: 6) alt rows, then
on foll 4th row. 88 (90: 92: 96: 98: 102) sts.
Cont straight until armhole measures 17 (18:
18: 19: 20: 21) cm, ending with a WS row.

Shape shoulders and back neck

Cast off 8 (8: 9: 9: 9: 10) sts at beg of next
2 rows. 72 (74: 74: 78: 80: 82) sts.
Next row (RS): Cast off 8 (8: 9: 9: 9: 10) sts,
patt until there are 13 (13: 12: 13: 14: 14) sts
on right needle and turn, leaving rem sts on
a holder.
Work each side of neck separately.
Cast off 4 sts at beg of next row.
Cast off rem 9 (9: 8: 9: 10: 10) sts.
With RS facing, rejoin yarn to rem sts, cast off
centre 30 (32: 32: 34: 34: 34) sts, patt to end.
Complete to match first side, reversing shapings.

LEFT FRONT

Cast on 54 (57: 61: 64: 68: 73) sts using
2mm (US 0) needles.
Beg and ending rows as indicated, working
chart rows 1 to 10 **once only** and then
repeating chart rows 11 to 22 **throughout**,
cont in patt from chart as folls:
Work 10 rows, ending with a WS row.
Change to 2¾mm (US 2) needles.

Keeping patt correct, dec 1 st at beg of
15th and 2 foll 8th rows, then on 4 foll
6th rows.
47 (50: 54: 57: 61: 66) sts.
Cont straight until left front measures 21 (21:
22: 22: 22: 22) cm, ending with a WS row.
Inc 1 st at beg of next and 3 foll 10th
rows, then on 3 foll 12th rows, taking
inc sts into patt.
54 (57: 61: 64: 68: 73) sts.
Work 2 rows, ending with a RS row.

Shape front neck

Keeping patt correct, cast off 14 (15: 15: 16:
16: 16) sts at beg of next row.
40 (42: 46: 48: 52: 57) sts.
Dec 1 st at neck edge of next 9 rows.
31 (33: 37: 39: 43: 48) sts.
Work 1 row, ending with a WS row.

Shape armhole

Keeping patt correct, cast off 4 (4: 5: 5: 6: 6)
sts at beg and dec 1 st at end of next row.
26 (28: 31: 33: 36: 41) sts.
Work 1 row.
Dec 1 st at armhole edge of next 3 (5: 5: 7:
7: 9) rows, then on foll 2 (2: 4: 3: 5: 6) alt
rows, then on foll 4th row **and at same time**
dec 1 st at neck edge of next and 2 foll 4th
rows. 17 (17: 18: 19: 20: 22) sts.
Cont straight until 50 rows less have been
worked than on back to start of shoulder
shaping, ending with a WS row.
Inc 1 st at neck edge of next and 7 foll 6th
rows, taking inc sts into patt.
25 (25: 26: 27: 28: 30) sts.
Work 7 rows, ending with a WS row.

Shape shoulder

Cast off 8 (8: 9: 9: 9: 10) sts at beg of next
and foll alt row.
Work 1 row.
Cast off rem 9 (9: 8: 9: 10: 10) sts.

RIGHT FRONT

Cast on 54 (57: 61: 64: 68: 73) sts using
2mm (US 0) needles.
Beg and ending rows as indicated, working
chart rows 1 to 10 **once only** and then
repeating chart rows 11 to 22 **throughout**,
cont in patt from chart as folls:
Work 10 rows, ending with a WS row.
Change to 2¾mm (US 2) needles.

Keeping patt correct, dec 1 st at end of 15th and 2 foll 8th rows, then on 4 foll 6th rows.
47 (50: 54: 57: 61: 66) sts.
Complete to match left front, reversing shapings.

SLEEVES (both alike)
Cast on 66 (68: 70: 72: 74: 76) sts using 2mm (US 0) needles.
Beg and ending rows as indicated, working chart rows 1 to 10 **once only** and then repeating chart rows 11 to 22 **throughout**, cont in patt from chart as folls:
Work 10 rows, ending with a WS row.
Change to 2¾mm (US 2) needles.
Cont in patt, shaping sides by inc 1 st at each end of 11th and every foll 12th row to 84 (82: 80: 78: 90: 88) sts, then on 0 (2: 4: 6: 2: 4) foll 14th rows, taking inc sts into patt.
84 (86: 88: 90: 94: 96) sts.
Cont straight until sleeve measures 33 (34: 35: 36: 37: 38) cm, ending with a WS row.

Shape top
Keeping patt correct, cast off 4 (4: 5: 5: 6: 6) sts at beg of next 2 rows.
76 (78: 78: 80: 82: 84) sts.
Dec 1 st at each end of next 3 rows, then on foll alt row, then on foll 4th row, then on 5 foll 6th rows.
56 (58: 58: 60: 62: 64) sts.
Work 3 rows.
Dec 1 st at each end of next and every foll alt row to 50 sts, then on foll 7 rows, ending with a WS row.
Cast off rem 36 sts.

MAKING UP
Press all pieces with a warm iron over a damp cloth.
Join both shoulder seams using back stitch or mattress stitch if preferred.

Front opening and neck edging
With RS facing and using 2.50mm (US C2) crochet hook, attach yarn at base of right front opening edge, 1 ch (does NOT count as st), work 1 row of dc evenly up right front opening edge, around entire neck edge, and then down left front opening edge to cast-on edge.
Fasten off.
Mark positions for 13 buttonholes along right front opening edge - first to come 12 rows up from cast-on edge, last to come just below neck shaping, and rem 11 buttonholes evenly spaced between.
With RS facing and using 2.50mm (US C2) crochet hook, attach yarn to first dc of previous row of crochet, 1 ch (does NOT count as st),

work up right front opening edge as folls:
1 dc into each dc, making buttonholes to correspond with positions marked by replacing (1 dc into next dc) with (2 ch, miss 1 dc) and ending with 3 dc into dc at top of right front opening edge (place marker on centre dc of this group of 3 dc), now work 1 row of dc evenly around neck edge, missing dc as required to ensure edging lays flat, ending with 3 dc into dc at top of left front opening edge (place marker on centre dc of this group of 3 dc) and ensuring number of dc between marked dc is divisible by 5, then work 1 dc into each dc down left front opening edge.
Fasten off.
With RS facing and using 2.50mm (US C2) crochet hook, attach yarn to marked dc at top of right front opening edge by working a ss into this dc, *1 dc into next dc, 1 dc into next dc, 1 tr into next dc, 1 dc into next dc, 1 ss into next dc, rep from * to next marked dc, 1 ss into this marked dc.
Fasten off.
Join side seams. Join sleeve seams.
Insert sleeves into armholes. Sew on buttons.

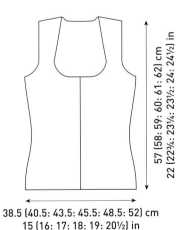

57 (58: 59: 60: 61: 62) cm
22 (22¾: 23¼: 23½: 24: 24½) in

38.5 (40.5: 43.5: 45.5: 48.5: 52) cm
15 (16: 17: 18: 19: 20½) in

33 (34: 35: 36: 37: 38) cm
13 (13¼: 13¾: 14¼: 14½: 15) in

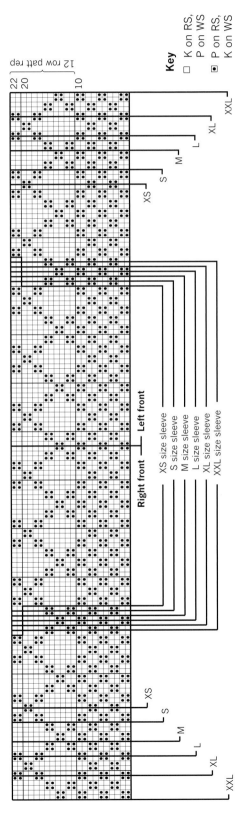

Key

□ K on RS, P on WS
▣ P on RS, K on WS

12 row patt rep

AZURE

Long-line boyfriend cardigan

Recommendation

Suitable for the knitter with a little experience
Please see pages 12 & 13 for photographs.

	XS	S	M	L	XL	XXL	
To fit	**81**	**86**	**91**	**97**	**102**	**109**	cm
bust	32	34	36	38	40	43	in

Rowan Creative Linen

	5	6	6	7	7	8 x 100gm

Photographed in Darkness

Needles

1 pair 4mm (no 8) (US 6) needles
1 pair 5mm (no 6) (US 8) needles

Buttons – 6

Tension

18 sts and 24 rows to 10 cm measured over
stocking stitch using 5mm (US 8) needles.

BACK

Cast on 88 (92: 96: 102: 106: 112) sts using
4mm (US 6) needles.
Row 1 (RS): K1 (0: 1: 0: 0: 1), P2 (1: 2: 2: 0:
2), *K2, P2, rep from * to last 1 (3: 1: 0: 2: 1)
sts, K1 (2: 1: 0: 2: 1), P0 (1: 0: 0: 0: 0).
Row 2: P1 (0: 1: 0: 0: 1), K2 (1: 2: 2: 0: 2),
*P2, K2, rep from * to last 1 (3: 1: 0: 2: 1) sts,
P1 (2: 1: 0: 2: 1), K0 (1: 0: 0: 0: 0).
These 2 rows form rib.
Work in rib for a further 18 rows, ending with
a WS row.
Change to 5mm (US 8) needles.
Starting with a K row, now work in st st as folls:
Work straight until back measures 58 (58: 59:
59: 59: 59) cm, ending with a WS row.
Shape armholes
Cast off 4 (4: 5: 5: 6: 6) sts at beg of next
2 rows. 80 (84: 86: 92: 94: 100) sts.
Dec 1 st at each end of next 3 (5: 5: 7: 7: 9)
rows, then on foll 6 (5: 5: 5: 5: 5) alt rows, then
on foll 4th row. 60 (62: 64: 66: 68: 70) sts.
Cont straight until armhole measures 21 (22:
22: 23: 24: 25) cm, ending with a WS row.
Shape shoulders and back neck
Next row (RS): Cast off 5 (5: 5: 5: 5: 6) sts,
K until there are 11 (11: 12: 12: 13: 13) sts
on right needle and turn, leaving rem sts on
a holder.
Work each side of neck separately.
Dec 1 st at neck edge of next row.
Cast off 5 (5: 5: 5: 5: 6) sts at beg and dec
1 st at end of next row.
Work 1 row.
Cast off rem 4 (4: 5: 5: 6: 5) sts.
With RS facing, rejoin yarn to rem sts, cast off
centre 28 (30: 30: 32: 32: 32) sts, K to end.
Complete to match first side, reversing shapings.

POCKET LININGS (make 2)

Cast on 25 (25: 27: 27: 29: 29) sts using 5mm
(US 8) needles.
Beg with a K row, work in st st for 28 rows,
ending with a WS row.
Break yarn and leave sts on a holder.

Pattern note: Row-end edges of fronts forms
actual front opening edges. To ensure edges
remains neat and tidy, make sure new balls of
yarn are joined in at side seam edges **only**.

LEFT FRONT

Cast on 49 (51: 53: 56: 58: 61) sts using
4mm (US 6) needles.
Row 1 (RS): K1 (0: 1: 0: 0: 1), P2 (1: 2: 2: 0:
2), *K2, P2, rep from * to last 10 sts, K10.
Row 2: K8, *P2, K2, rep from * to last 1 (3: 1:
0: 2: 1) sts, P1 (2: 1: 0: 2: 1), K0 (1: 0: 0: 0: 0).
These 2 rows set the sts - front opening edge
8 sts in g st with all other sts in rib.
Cont as set for a further 18 rows, ending with
a WS row.
Change to 5mm (US 8) needles.
Next row (RS): Knit.
Next row: K8, P to end.
These 2 rows set the sts - front opening edge
8 sts still in g st with all other sts now in st st.
Cont as set for a further 26 rows, ending with
a WS row.
Place pocket
Next row (RS): K7 (8: 8: 9: 9: 10), slip next
25 (25: 27: 27: 29: 29) sts onto a holder and, in
their place, K across 25 (25: 27: 27: 29: 29) sts
of first pocket lining, K17 (18: 18: 20: 20: 22).
Cont straight until 34 rows less have been
worked than on back to start of armhole
shaping, ending with a WS row.
Shape front slope
Next row (RS): K to last 10 sts, K2tog tbl, K8.
Working all front slope decreases as set by last
row, dec 1 st at front slope edge of 6th (6th: 6th:
4th: 6th: 6th) and 4 foll 6th rows.
43 (45: 47: 50: 52: 55) sts.
Work 3 (3: 3: 5: 3: 3) rows, ending with a WS row.
Shape armhole
Cast off 4 (4: 5: 5: 6: 6) sts at beg and dec
0 (0: 0: 1: 0: 0) st at end of next row.
39 (41: 42: 44: 46: 49) sts.
Work 1 row.
Dec 1 st at armhole edge of next 3 (5: 5: 7: 7:
9) rows, then on foll 6 (5: 5: 5: 5: 5) alt rows,
then on foll 4th row **and at same time** dec 1 st
at front slope edge of next (next: next: 5th: next:
next) and 3 (3: 3: 2: 3: 3) foll 6th rows.
25 (26: 27: 28: 29: 30) sts.
Dec 1 st at front slope edge **only** on 6th (6th:
6th: 2nd: 4th: 2nd) and 0 (3: 3: 4: 4: 3) foll
6th rows, then on 2 (0: 0: 0: 0: 1) foll 8th rows.
22 (22: 23: 23: 24: 25) sts.
Cont straight until left front matches back to
start of shoulder shaping, ending with a WS row.

Shape shoulder

Cast off 5 (5: 5: 5: 5: 6) sts at beg of next and foll alt row.

Next row (WS): K8, M1, P to end.

Cast off 4 (4: 5: 5: 6: 5) sts at beg of next row. 9 sts.

Cont in g st on these 9 sts for a further 8.5 (9: 9: 9.5: 9.5: 9.5) cm (for back neck border extension), ending with a WS row.

Cast off.

Mark positions for 6 buttons along left front opening edge - first button to come level with row 5, 6th button to come 2 cm below start of front slope shaping, and rem 4 buttons evenly spaced between.

RIGHT FRONT

Cast on 49 (51: 53: 56: 58: 61) sts using 4mm (US 6) needles.

Row 1 (RS): K8, *K2, P2, rep from * to last 1 (3: 1: 0: 2: 1) sts, K1 (2: 1: 0: 2: 1), P0 (1: 0: 0: 0: 0).

Row 2: P1 (0: 1: 0: 0: 1), K2 (1: 2: 2: 0: 2), *P2, K2, rep from * to last 10 sts, P2, K8.

These 2 rows set the sts - front opening edge 8 sts in g st with all other sts in rib.

Cont as set for a further 2 rows, ending with a WS row.

Row 5 (buttonhole row) (RS): K2, K2tog tbl, (yfwd) twice, K2tog (to make a buttonhole - on next row, work into back and front in double yfwd of this row), patt to end.

Making a further 5 buttonholes in this way to correspond with positions marked for buttons on left front and noting that no further reference will be made to buttonholes, cont as folls:

Work 15 rows, ending with a WS row.

Change to 5mm (US 8) needles.

Next row (RS): Knit.

Next row: P to last 8 sts, K8.

These 2 rows set the sts - front opening edge 8 sts still in g st with all other sts now in st st.

Cont as set for a further 26 rows, ending with a WS row.

Place pocket

Next row (RS): K17 (18: 18: 20: 20: 22), slip next 25 (25: 27: 27: 29: 29) sts onto a holder and, in their place, K across 25 (25: 27: 27: 29: 29) sts of second pocket lining, K7 (8: 8: 9: 9: 10).

Cont straight until 34 rows less have been worked than on back to start of armhole shaping, ending with a WS row.

Shape front slope

Next row (RS): K8, K2tog, K to end.

Working all front slope decreases as set by last row, complete to match left front, reversing shapings.

SLEEVES (both alike)

Cast on 34 (36: 36: 38: 40: 42) sts using 4mm (US 6) needles.

Row 1 (RS): K0 (0: 0: 0: 1: 0), P0 (1: 1: 2: 2: 0), *K2, P2, rep from * to last 2 (3: 3: 0: 1: 2) sts, K2 (2: 2: 0: 1: 2), P0 (1: 1: 0: 0: 0).

Row 2: P0 (0: 0: 0: 1: 0), K0 (1: 1: 2: 2: 0), *P2, K2, rep from * to last 2 (3: 3: 0: 1: 2) sts, P2 (2: 2: 0: 1: 2), K0 (1: 1: 0: 0: 0).

These 2 rows form rib.

Cont in rib, inc 1 st at each end of 9th and foll 10th (10th: 10th: 10th: 12th: 12th) row. 38 (40: 40: 42: 44: 46) sts.

Work in rib for a further 9 (9: 9: 9: 7: 7) rows, ending with a WS row.

Change to 5mm (US 8) needles.

Starting with a K row, now work in st st as folls:

Work 0 (0: 0: 2: 4: 4) rows, ending with a WS row.

Next row (RS): K3, M1, K to last 3 sts, M1, K3.

Working all sleeve increases as set by last row, inc 1 st at each end of 10th (10th: 10th: 12th: 12th: 12th) and every foll 10th (10th: 12th: 12th: 12th: 12th) row to 46 (46: 56: 58: 60: 60) sts, then on every foll 12th (12th: -: -: -: 14th) row until there are 54 (56: -: -: -: 62) sts.

Cont straight until sleeve measures 50 (51: 52: 53: 54: 55) cm, ending with a WS row.

Shape top

Cast off 4 (4: 5: 5: 6: 6) sts at beg of next 2 rows. 46 (48: 46: 48: 48: 50) sts.

Dec 1 st at each end of next and foll alt row, then on 5 (5: 6: 6: 7: 7) foll 4th rows. 32 (34: 30: 32: 30: 32) sts.

Work 1 row.

Dec 1 st at each end of next and foll 1 (2: 0: 1: 0: 1) alt rows, then on foll 5 rows, ending with a WS row.

Cast off rem 18 sts.

MAKING UP

Press all pieces with a warm iron over a damp cloth.

Join both shoulder seams using back stitch or mattress stitch if preferred. Join cast-off ends of back neck border extensions, then sew one edge in place to back neck.

Pocket tops (both alike)

Slip 25 (25: 27: 27: 29: 29) sts from pocket holder onto 4mm (US 6) needles and rejoin yarn with RS facing.

Starting with a K row, now work in st st for 6 rows, ending with a WS row.

Cast off.

Join side seams. Join sleeve seams. Insert sleeves into armholes. Sew pocket linings in place on inside, then neatly sew down ends of pocket tops, allowing them to roll to RS. Sew on buttons.

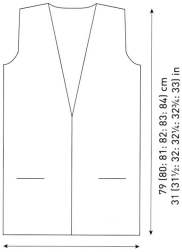

79 (80: 81: 82: 83: 84) cm
31 (31½: 32: 32¼: 32¾: 33) in

48 (50.5: 53: 55.5: 58: 62) cm
19 (20: 21: 22: 23: 24½) in

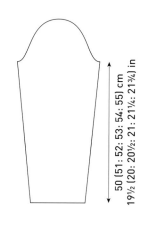

50 (51: 52: 53: 54: 55) cm
19½ (20: 20½: 21: 21¼: 21¾) in

ZEST
Fitted cap sleeved top with side vents

Recommendation

Suitable for the knitter with a little experience
Please see pages 14 & 15 for photographs.

	XS	S	M	L	XL	XXL	
To fit	81	86	91	97	102	109	cm
hips	32	34	36	38	40	43	in

Rowan Siena 4 ply

7 7 8 8 9 9 x 50gm

Photographed in Greengage

Needles

1 pair 2mm (no 14) (US 0) needles
1 pair 2¼mm (no 13) (US 1) needles
1 pair 2¾mm (no 12) (US 2) needles
2.50mm (no 12) (US C2) crochet hook

Tension

28 sts and 42 rows to 10 cm measured over
pattern using 2¾mm (US 2) needles.

Crochet abbreviations

ch = chain; **dc** = double crochet; **ss** = slip
stitch; **tr** = treble.
See page 99 for further details.

BACK

Lower border

Cast on 24 sts using 2mm (US 0) needles.
Row 1 (RS): Knit.
Rows 2 and 3: Purl.
Row 4: Knit.
These 4 rows form ribbed patt.
Cont in ribbed patt until border, unstretched,
measures approx 38 (40: 43: 45: 48: 52) cm,
ending after patt row 2 and with a WS row.
Cast off but do NOT break yarn.

Main section

With RS facing and using 2¾mm (US 2)
needles, pick up and knit 106 (112: 120: 126:
134: 144) sts evenly along one row-end edge
of lower border.
Next row (WS): Purl.
Beg and ending rows as indicated and
repeating the 12 row patt rep throughout,
cont in patt from chart as folls:
Work 2 rows, ending with a WS row.
Keeping patt correct, dec 1 st at each end of
next and foll 8th row, then on 4 foll 6th rows.
94 (100: 108: 114: 122: 132) sts.
Cont straight until back measures 21 (21:
22: 22: 22: 22) cm from lower edge of hem
border, ending with a WS row.
Inc 1 st at each end of next and 3 foll 10th
rows, then on 3 foll 12th rows, taking inc sts
into patt. 108 (114: 122: 128: 136: 146) sts.
Work 13 rows, ending with a WS row.

Shape armholes

Keeping patt correct, cast off 4 (4: 5: 5: 6: 6)
sts at beg of next 2 rows.
100 (106: 112: 118: 124: 134) sts.
Dec 1 st at each end of next 3 (5: 5: 7: 7: 9)
rows, then on foll 2 (2: 4: 3: 5: 6) alt rows, then
on foll 4th row. 88 (90: 92: 96: 98: 102) sts.
Cont straight until armhole measures 17 (18:
18: 19: 20: 21) cm, ending with a WS row.

Shape shoulders and back neck

Cast off 8 (8: 9: 9: 9: 10) sts at beg of next 2
rows. 72 (74: 74: 78: 80: 82) sts.
Next row (RS): Cast off 8 (8: 9: 9: 9: 10) sts,
patt until there are 13 (13: 12: 13: 14: 14) sts
on right needle and turn, leaving rem sts on a
holder.
Work each side of neck separately.
Cast off 4 sts at beg of next row.
Cast off rem 9 (9: 8: 9: 10: 10) sts.

With RS facing, rejoin yarn to rem sts, cast off
centre 30 (32: 32: 34: 34: 34) sts, patt to end.
Complete to match first side, reversing
shapings.

FRONT

Work as given for back until 10 rows less have
been worked than on back to start of armhole
shaping, ending with a WS row.

Shape front neck

Next row (RS): Patt 39 (41: 45: 47: 51: 56)
sts and turn, leaving rem sts on a holder.
Work each side of neck separately.
Keeping patt correct, dec 1 st at neck edge
of next 8 rows.
31 (33: 37: 39: 43: 48) sts.
Work 1 row, ending with a WS row.

Shape armhole

Keeping patt correct, cast off 4 (4: 5: 5: 6: 6)
sts at beg and dec 1 st at end of next row.
26 (28: 31: 33: 36: 41) sts.
Work 1 row.
Dec 1 st at armhole edge of next 3 (5: 5: 7:
7: 9) rows, then on foll 2 (2: 4: 3: 5: 6) alt
rows, then on foll 4th row **and at same time**
dec 1 st at neck edge of next and 2 foll 4th
rows.
17 (17: 18: 19: 20: 22) sts.
Cont straight until 50 rows less have been
worked than on back to start of shoulder
shaping, ending with a WS row.
Inc 1 st at neck edge of next and 7 foll 6th
rows, taking inc sts into patt.
25 (25: 26: 27: 28: 30) sts.
Work 7 rows, ending with a WS row.

Shape shoulder

Cast off 8 (8: 9: 9: 9: 10) sts at beg of next
and foll alt row.
Work 1 row.
Cast off rem 9 (9: 8: 9: 10: 10) sts.
With RS facing, rejoin yarn to rem sts, cast off
centre 30 (32: 32: 34: 34: 34) sts, patt to end.
Complete to match first side, reversing
shapings.

SLEEVES (both alike)

Cast on 7 sts using 2¼mm (US 1) needles.
Beg with patt row 1, work in ribbed patt as
given for back hem border as folls:
Work 12 rows, ending with a WS row.

Inc 1 st at beg of next and 3 foll 4th rows,
then on foll 6 alt rows, then on 2 foll 4th rows,
taking inc sts into patt. 19 sts.
Work 40 (44: 44: 48: 52: 56) rows, ending
with a RS row.
Place marker at beg of last row - this will
match to shoulder seam.
Work 41 (45: 45: 49: 53: 57) rows, ending
with a WS row.
Dec 1 st at beg of next and 2 foll 4th rows,
then on foll 6 alt rows, then on 3 foll 4th rows.
7 sts.
Work a further 11 rows, ending after patt row
2 and a WS row.
Cast off.

MAKING UP
Press all pieces with a warm iron over
a damp cloth.
Join both shoulder seams using back stitch
or mattress stitch if preferred.
Neck edging
With RS facing and using 2.50mm (US C2)
crochet hook, attach yarn to neck edge at
left shoulder seam, 1 ch (does NOT count as
st), work 1 round of dc evenly around entire
neck edge, ensuring number of dc worked is
divisible by 5 and ending with ss to first dc,
do NOT turn.
Next round (RS): Miss first dc, *1 dc into
next dc, 1 tr into next dc, 1 dc into next dc**,
1 ss into each of next 2 dc, rep from * to end,
ending last rep at **, 1 ss into last dc.
Fasten off.
Join side seams, leaving seams open along
cast-on and cast-off edges of hem borders.
Join cast-on and cast-off edges of sleeves to
form sleeve seams. Insert sleeves into armholes,
matching sleeve marker to shoulder seam.

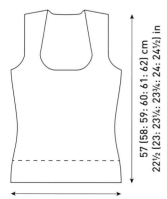

57 (58: 59: 60: 61: 62) cm
22½ (23: 23¼: 23¾: 24: 24½) in

38.5 (40.5: 43.5: 45.5: 48.5: 52) cm
15¼ (16: 17: 18: 19: 20½) in

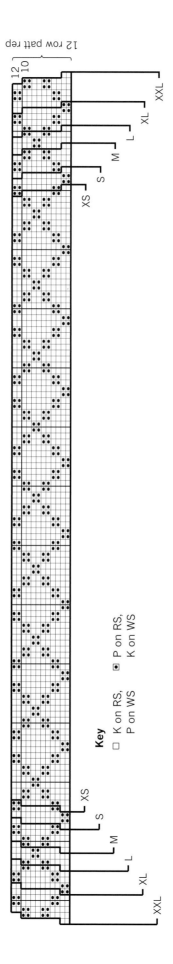

12 row patt rep

12
10

XXL
XL
L
M
S
XS

Key

□ K on RS,   ▣ P on RS,
P on WS   K on WS

XS
S
M
L
XL
XXL

COBALT
Zigzag textured cardigan

Recommendation
Suitable for the knitter with a little experience
Please see pages 8 & 9 for photographs.

	XS	S	M	L	XL	XXL	
To fit	**81**	**86**	**91**	**97**	**102**	**109**	**cm**
bust	32	34	36	38	40	43	in

Rowan Handknit Cotton
| | 10 | 11 | 11 | 12 | 12 | 13 | x 50gm |

Photographed in Thunder

Needles
1 pair 3¼mm (no 10) (US 3) needles
1 pair 3¾mm (no 9) (US 5) needles
1 pair 4mm (no 8) (US 6) needles

Buttons – 6

Tension
20 sts and 28 rows to 10 cm measured over pattern using 4mm (US 6) needles.

BACK
Cast on 83 (87: 93: 97: 103: 111) sts using 3¾mm (US 5) needles.
Beg and ending rows as indicated, noting that chart row 1 is a **WS** row, working chart rows 1 to 41 **once only** and then repeating chart rows 42 to 65 **throughout**, cont in patt from chart for back as folls:
Work 11 rows, ending with a WS row.
Change to 4mm (US 6) needles.
Keeping patt correct, dec 1 st at each end of 7th and 4 foll 6th rows.
73 (77: 83: 87: 93: 101) sts.
Work 19 (19: 21: 21: 21: 21) rows, ending with a WS row.
Inc 1 st at each end of next and 2 foll 8th rows, then on 2 foll 10th rows, taking inc sts into patt. 83 (87: 93: 97: 103: 111) sts.
Cont straight until back measures 38 (38: 39: 39: 39: 39) cm, ending with a WS row.

Shape armholes
Keeping patt correct, cast off 3 (4: 4: 5: 5: 6) sts at beg of next 2 rows. 77 (79: 85: 87: 93: 99) sts.
Dec 1 st at each end of next 3 (3: 5: 5: 7: 7) rows, then on foll 3 (3: 3: 3: 3: 4) alt rows, then on foll 4th row.
63 (65: 67: 69: 71: 75) sts.
Cont straight until armhole measures 18 (19: 19: 20: 21: 22) cm, ending with a WS row.

Shape shoulders and back neck
Cast off 5 (5: 5: 5: 5: 6) sts at beg of next 2 rows.
53 (55: 57: 59: 61: 63) sts.
Next row (RS): Cast off 5 (5: 5: 5: 5: 6) sts, patt until there are 8 (8: 9: 9: 10: 10) sts on right needle and turn, leaving rem sts on a holder.
Work each side of neck separately.
Cast off 4 sts at beg of next row.
Cast off rem 4 (4: 5: 5: 6: 6) sts.
With RS facing, rejoin yarn to rem sts, cast off centre 27 (29: 29: 31: 31: 31) sts, patt to end.
Complete to match first side, reversing shapings.

Pattern note: Row-end edges of fronts forms actual front opening edges. To ensure edges remains neat and tidy, make sure new balls of yarn are joined in at side seam edges **only**.

LEFT FRONT
Cast on 48 (50: 53: 55: 58: 62) sts using 3¾mm (US 5) needles.
Beg and ending rows as indicated, noting that chart row 1 is a **WS** row, working chart rows 1 to 41 **once only** and then repeating chart rows 42 to 65 **throughout**, cont in patt from chart for left front as folls:
Work 11 rows, ending with a WS row.
Change to 4mm (US 6) needles.
Keeping patt correct, dec 1 st at beg of 7th and 4 foll 6th rows. 43 (45: 48: 50: 53: 57) sts.
Work 19 (19: 21: 21: 21: 21) rows, ending with a WS row.
Inc 1 st at beg of next and 2 foll 8th rows, then on 2 foll 10th rows, taking inc sts into patt. 48 (50: 53: 55: 58: 62) sts.
Cont straight until left front matches back to start of armhole shaping, ending with a WS row.

Shape armhole
Keeping patt correct, cast off 3 (4: 4: 5: 5: 6) sts at beg of next row. 45 (46: 49: 50: 53: 56) sts.
Work 1 row.
Dec 1 st at armhole edge of next 3 (3: 5: 5: 7: 7) rows, then on foll 3 (3: 3: 3: 3: 4) alt rows, then on foll 4th row.
38 (39: 40: 41: 42: 44) sts.
Cont straight until 16 (16: 16: 18: 18: 18) rows less have been worked than on back to start of shoulder shaping, ending with a WS row.

Shape front neck
Next row (RS): Patt 24 (24: 25: 26: 27: 29) sts and turn, leaving rem 14 (15: 15: 15: 15: 15) sts on a holder.
Keeping patt correct, dec 1 st at neck edge of next 6 rows, then on foll 3 (3: 3: 4: 4: 4) alt rows. 15 (15: 16: 16: 17: 19) sts.
Work 3 rows, ending with RS facing for next row.

Shape shoulder
Cast off 5 (5: 5: 5: 5: 6) sts at beg of next and foll alt row **and at same time** dec 1 st at neck edge of next row.
Work 1 row.
Cast off rem 4 (4: 5: 5: 6: 6) sts.
Mark positions for 6 buttons along left front opening edge - first button to come level with row 28, 6th button to come level with first row of neck shaping, and rem 4 buttons evenly spaced between.

RIGHT FRONT

Cast on 48 (50: 53: 55: 58: 62) sts using 3¾mm (US 5) needles.

Beg and ending rows as indicated, noting that chart row 1 is a **WS** row, working chart rows 1 to 41 **once only** and then repeating charts rows 42 to 65 **throughout**, cont in patt from chart for right front as folls:

Work 11 rows, ending with a WS row.

Change to 4mm (US 6) needles.

Keeping patt correct, dec 1 st at end of 7th and foll 6th row.

46 (48: 51: 53: 56: 60) sts.

Work 3 rows, ending with a WS row.

Row 28 (buttonhole row) (RS): Patt 2 sts, work 2 tog tbl, yrn (to make a buttonhole), patt to end.

Making a further 5 buttonholes in this way to correspond with positions marked for buttons on left front and noting that no further reference will be made to buttonholes, cont as folls:

Keeping patt correct, dec 1 st at end of 2nd and 2 foll 6th rows.

43 (45: 48: 50: 53: 57) sts.

Complete to match left front, reversing shapings and working first row of neck shaping as folls:

Shape front neck

Next row (RS): Patt 2 sts, work 2 tog tbl, yrn (to make 6th buttonhole), patt 10 (11: 11: 11: 11: 11) sts and slip these 14 (15: 15: 15: 15: 15) sts onto a holder, patt to end.

24 (24: 25: 26: 27: 29) sts.

SLEEVES (both alike)

Cast on 49 (51: 51: 53: 55: 57) sts using 3¾mm (US 5) needles.

Beg and ending rows as indicated, noting that chart row 1 is a **WS** row, working chart rows 1 to 43 **once only** and then repeating chart rows 44 to 67 **throughout**, cont in patt from chart for sleeve as folls:

Work 11 rows, ending with a WS row.

Change to 4mm (US 6) needles.

Cont in patt, shaping sides by inc 1 st at each end of 7th and every foll 14th row to 61 (63: 61: 63: 65: 67) sts, then on 0 (0: 1: 1: 1: 1) foll 16th row, taking inc sts into patt.

61 (63: 63: 65: 67: 69) sts.

Cont straight until sleeve measures approx 34 (34: 35: 35: 35: 35) cm, ending at same point in patt as on back to beg of armhole shaping and with a WS row.

Shape top

Keeping patt correct, cast off 3 (4: 4: 5: 5: 6) sts at beg of next 2 rows.

55 (55: 55: 55: 57: 57) sts.

Back chart

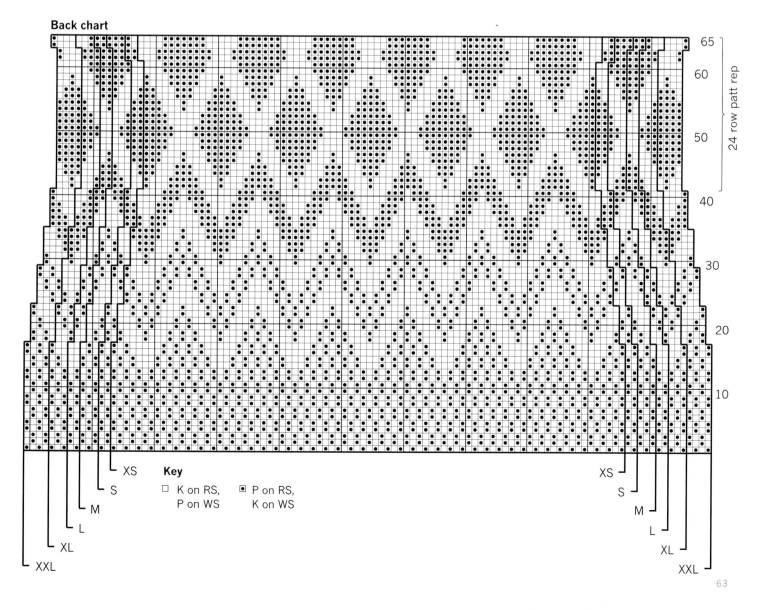

24 row patt rep

Key

□ K on RS, P on WS

▣ P on RS, K on WS

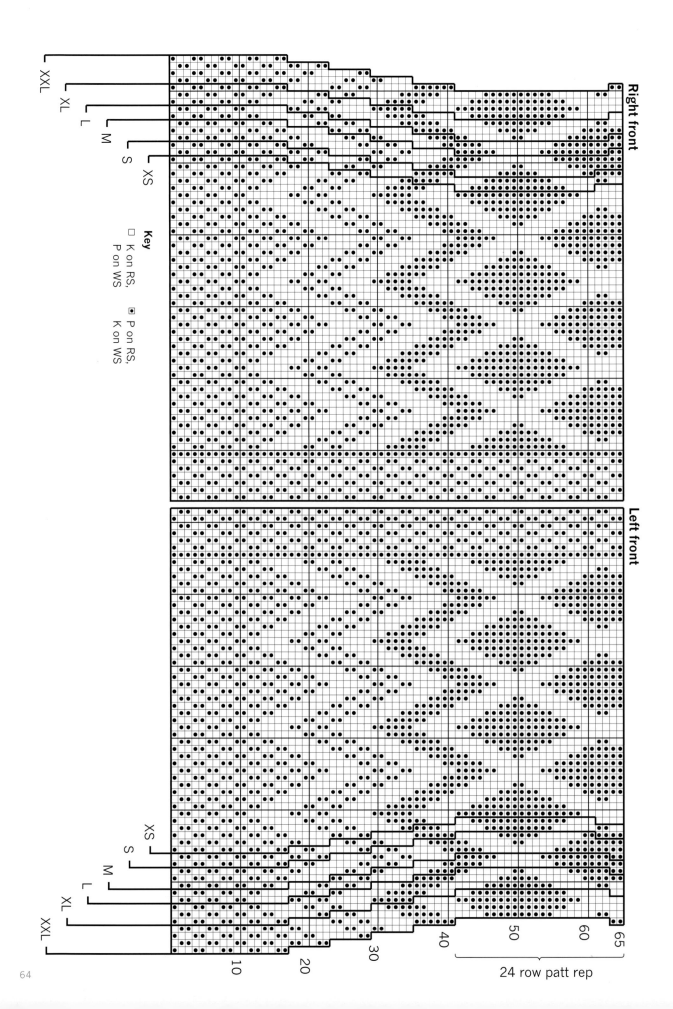

Right front

Left front

Key
☐ K on RS, P on WS
⊡ P on RS, K on WS

XXL
XL
L
M
S
XS

XS
S
M
L
XL
XXL

10
20
30
40
50
60
65

24 row patt rep

Dec 1 st at each end of next 3 rows, then on foll alt row, then on 4 (5: 5: 6: 6: 7) foll 4th rows. 39 (37: 37: 35: 37: 35) sts.
Work 1 row.
Dec 1 st at each end of next and foll 4 (3: 3: 2: 3: 2) alt rows, then on foll 5 rows, ending with a WS row.
Cast off rem 19 sts.

MAKING UP
Press all pieces with a warm iron over a damp cloth.
Join both shoulder seams using back stitch or mattress stitch if preferred.

Neckband
With RS facing and using 3¼mm (US 3) needles, slip 14 (15: 15: 15: 15: 15) sts on right front holder onto right needle, rejoin yarn and pick up and knit 18 (18: 18: 20: 20: 20) sts up right side of neck, 35 (37: 37: 39: 39: 39) sts from back, and 18 (18: 18: 20: 20: 20) sts down left side of neck, then patt 14 (15: 15: 15: 15: 15) sts on left front holder.
99 (103: 103: 109: 109: 109) sts.
Row 1 (WS): Patt 7 sts, *P1, K1, rep from * to last 8 sts, P1, patt 7 sts.
Row 2: Patt 7 sts, *K1, P1, rep from * to last 8 sts, K1, patt 7 sts.
Row 3: Patt 7 sts, *K1, P1, rep from * to last 8 sts, K1, patt 7 sts.
Row 4: Patt 7 sts, *P1, K1, rep from * to last 8 sts, P1, patt 7 sts.
These 4 rows set the sts - front opening edge 7 sts still in patt as set with all other sts in same patt as at lower edges.
Cont as set for a further 2 rows, ending with a RS row.
Cast off in patt (on **WS**).
Join side seams. Join sleeve seams.
Insert sleeves into armholes.
Sew on buttons.

56 (57: 58: 59: 60: 61) cm
22 (22½: 23: 23¼: 23¾: 24) in

41.5 (43.5: 46.6: 48.5: 51.5: 55.5) cm
16¼ (17: 18¼: 19: 20: 21¾) in

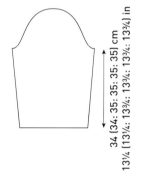

34 (34: 35: 35: 35: 35) cm
13¼ (13¼: 13¾: 13¾: 13¾: 13¾) in

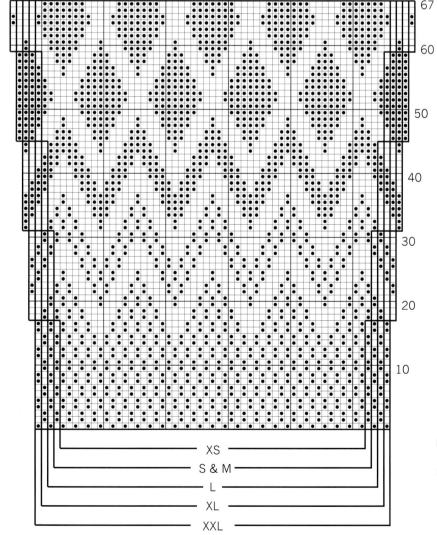

67
60
50
40
30
20
10

XS
S & M
L
XL
XXL

Key
☐ K on RS, P on WS
▣ P on RS, K on WS

BITTER
Close fitting sculpted vest

Recommendation
Suitable for the more experienced knitter
Please see pages 16 & 17 for photographs.

	XS	S	M	L	XL	XXL	
To fit	**81**	**86**	**91**	**97**	**102**	**109**	cm
bust	32	34	36	38	40	43	in

Rowan Creative Linen
3	3	4	4	4	5 x 100gm

Photographed in Eggplant

Needles
1 pair 3¾mm (no 9) (US 5) needles

Tension
23 sts and 33 rows to 10 cm measured over
pattern using 3¾mm (US 5) needles.

BACK
Cast on 55 (63: 71: 79: 87: 95) sts using
3¾mm (US 5) needles.
Row 1 (RS): K5, P1, *K3, P1, rep from * to last
5 sts, K5.
Counting in from both ends of last row, place
marker after 9th st in from ends of rows.
Row 2: (K3, P1) twice, K1, slip marker onto
right needle, M1, K2, *P1, K3, rep from * to
last 12 sts, P1, K2, M1, slip marker onto right
needle, K1, (P1, K3) twice.
These 2 rows set the sts - 3 st g st and patt
borders with all other sts in patt.
Keeping patt correct and taking inc sts into
patt, cont as folls:
Row 3: Patt to marker, slip marker onto right
needle, M1, patt to next marker, M1, slip
marker onto right needle, patt to end.
Working all increases as set by last row, inc 1
st at each end of next 2 rows, then on foll 6 alt
rows, then on 6 foll 4th rows, taking inc sts into
patt. 87 (95: 103: 111: 119: 127) sts.
Now working **all** sts in patt, cont as folls:
Work 11 (11: 13: 13: 13: 13) rows, ending
with a WS row.
Next row (dec) (RS): Patt to marker, slip
marker onto right needle, work 2 tog, patt to
within 2 sts of next marker, work 2 tog tbl, slip
marker onto right needle, patt 9 sts.
Keeping patt correct and working all decreases
as set by last row, dec 1 st at each end of 4th
and 6 foll 4th rows.
71 (79: 87: 95: 103: 111) sts.
Work 13 (13: 15: 15: 15: 15) rows, ending with
a WS row.
Next row (inc) (RS): Patt to marker, slip
marker onto right needle, M1, patt to next
marker, M1, slip marker onto right needle, patt
to end.**
Keeping patt correct and working all increases
as set by last row, inc 1 st at each end of 6th
and 6 foll 6th rows.
87 (95: 103: 111: 119: 127) sts.
Work 7 rows, ending with a WS row.
Shape armholes
Keeping patt correct, cast off 4 (4: 4: 4: 8: 8)
sts at beg of next row.
Next row (WS): Cast off 4 (4: 4: 4: 8: 8) sts -
one st on right needle, K2, patt to last 3 sts, K3.
79 (87: 95: 103: 103: 111) sts.

Next row (RS): K5, P2tog, patt to last 7 sts,
P2tog tbl, K5.
Next row: K3, P1, K1, K2tog tbl, patt to last
7 sts, K2tog, K1, P1, K3.
Last 2 rows set the sts - decreases worked 7
sts in from armhole edges and armhole edge
3 sts worked in g st, with all other sts worked
in patt as set.
Keeping sts correct as now set and working all
armhole decreases as set by last 2 rows, dec
1 st at each end of next 3 (5: 7: 7: 7: 9) rows,
then on foll 1 (3: 4: 5: 5: 7) alt rows, then on
1 (1: 0: 0: 1: 0) foll 4th row.
65 (65: 69: 75: 73: 75) sts.
Work 3 (1: 1: 1: 1: 3) rows, ending with
a WS row.
Place marker on centre st of last row.
Next row (RS): (K5, P2tog) 0 (0: 1: 0: 0: 1)
times, patt to within 3 sts of marked st, K7
(marked st is centre st of these 7 sts), patt to
last 0 (0: 7: 0: 0: 7) sts, (P2tog tbl, K5) 0 (0: 1:
0: 0: 1) times. 65 (65: 67: 75: 73: 73) sts.
Next row: Patt to within 3 sts of marked st, K7
(marked st is centre st of these 7 sts), patt to
end.
These 2 rows set centre 7 sts now worked in
g st instead of patt.
Keeping sts correct as now set, cont as folls:
Work 2 rows, dec 1 (0: 0: 1: 0: 0) st at each
end of first of these rows and ending with
a WS row. 63 (65: 67: 73: 73: 73) sts.
Divide for back neck
Next row (RS): (K5, P2tog) 0 (1: 1: 0: 1: 0)
times, patt to marked st and turn, leaving
marked st and rem 31 (32: 33: 36: 36: 36) sts
on a holder.
31 (31: 32: 36: 35: 36) sts.
Work each side of neck separately.
Working all back neck decreases in same way
as armhole decrease, dec 1 st at back neck
edge of 2nd and foll 15 alt rows **and at same
time** dec 0 (0: 1: 1: 0: 1) st at armhole edge
of 0 (0: 6th: 4th: 0: 2nd) row.
15 (15: 15: 19: 19: 19) sts.
Work 3 rows, ending with a WS row.
Shape shoulder
Cast off 5 (5: 5: 6: 6: 6) sts at beg of next and
foll alt row.
Work 1 row.
Cast off rem 5 (5: 5: 7: 7: 7) sts.

With RS facing, rejoin yarn to rem sts, K2tog, patt to last 0 (7: 7: 0: 7: 0) sts, (P2tog tbl, K5) 0 (1: 1: 0: 1: 0) times.
31 (31: 32: 36: 35: 36) sts.
Complete to match first side, reversing shapings.

FRONT
Work as given for back to **.
Keeping patt correct and working all increases as set by last row, inc 1 st at each end of 6th and 5 foll 6th rows.
85 (93: 101: 109: 117: 125) sts.
Work 1 row, ending with a WS row.
Place marker on centre st of last row.
Next row (RS): Patt to within 3 sts of centre marked st, K7 (marked st is centre st of these 7 sts), patt to end.
Next row: Patt to within 3 sts of marked st, K7 (marked st is centre st of these 7 sts), patt to end.
These 2 rows set centre 7 sts now worked in g st instead of patt.
Keeping sts correct as now set, cont as folls:
Work 2 rows, ending with a WS row.
Divide for front neck
Next row (RS): Patt 9 sts, M1, patt to centre marked st and turn, leaving marked st and rem 42 (46: 50: 54: 58: 62) sts on a holder. 43 (47: 51: 55: 59: 63) sts.
Work each side of neck separately.
Working all front neck decreases in same way as back armhole and neck decreases, dec 1 st at front neck edge of 2nd (4th: 4th: 4th: 4th: 4th) and foll 1 (0: 0: 0: 0: 0) alt row.
41 (46: 50: 54: 58: 62) sts.
Work 3 rows, ending with a WS row.
Shape armhole
Keeping patt correct, cast off 4 (4: 4: 4: 8: 8) sts at beg and dec 1 st at end of next row.
36 (41: 45: 49: 49: 53) sts.
Now working armhole edge 3 sts in g st and armhole decreases in same way as given for back, cont as folls:
Work 1 row.
Dec 1 st at armhole edge of next 5 (7: 9: 9: 9: 11) rows, then on foll 1 (3: 5: 5: 5: 7) alt rows, then on foll 4th row, then on foll 6th row **and at same time** dec 1 st at front neck edge of 3rd and 3 (5: 6: 6: 6: 8) foll 4th rows.
24 (23: 22: 26: 26: 24) sts.
Dec 1 st at front neck edge **only** on 2nd (4th: 2nd: 2nd: 2nd: 4th) row and 8 (7: 6: 6: 4: 0) foll 4th rows, then on 0 (0: 0: 0: 2: 4) foll 6th rows. 15 (15: 15: 19: 19: 19) sts.
Work 3 (3: 3: 5: 5: 5) rows, ending with a WS row.

Shape shoulder
Cast off 5 (5: 5: 6: 6: 6) sts at beg of next and foll alt row.
Work 1 row.
Cast off rem 5 (5: 5: 7: 7: 7) sts.
With RS facing, rejoin yarn to rem sts, K2tog, patt to last 9 sts, M1, patt 9 sts. 43 (47: 51: 55: 59: 63) sts.
Complete to match first side, reversing shapings.

MAKING UP
Press all pieces with a warm iron over a damp cloth.
Join both shoulder seams using back stitch or mattress stitch if preferred. Join side seams, leaving seams open for first 40 rows.

61 (62: 63: 64: 65: 66) cm
24 (24 ½: 24 ¾: 25 ¼: 25 ¾: 26) in

38 (41.5: 45: 48.5: 51.5: 55) cm
15 (16½: 17¾: 19: 20¼: 21½) in

BURNT
Fitted slip stitch ribbed vest

Recommendation
Suitable for the knitter with a little experience
Please see pages 28, 29 & 30 for photographs.

	XS	S	M	L	XL	XXL	
To fit	**81**	**86**	**91**	**97**	**102**	**109**	cm
bust	32	34	36	38	40	43	in

Rowan Cotton Glace
6   6   7   7   8   8   x 50gm
Photographed in Baked Red

Needles
1 pair 2¾mm (no 12) (US 2) needles
1 pair 3¼mm (no 10) (US 3) needles

Buttons – 1

Tension
28 sts and 38 rows to 10 cm measured over
pattern using 3¼mm (US 3) needles.

FRONT
Cast on 107 (113: 121: 127: 135: 145) sts
using 2¾mm (US 2) needles.
Row 1 (RS): K3 (1: 5: 3: 2: 2), slip next st
purlwise with yarn at back (WS) of work, *K4,
slip next st purlwise with yarn at back (WS)
of work, rep from * to last 3 (1: 5: 3: 2: 2) sts,
K3 (1: 5: 3: 2: 2).
Row 2: K3 (1: 5: 3: 2: 2), P1, *K4, P1, rep from
* to last 3 (1: 5: 3: 2: 2) sts, K3 (1: 5: 3: 2: 2).
Rep last 2 rows twice more.
Change to 3¼mm (US 3) needles.
Now work in patt as folls:
Row 1 (RS): P3 (1: 5: 3: 2: 2), slip next st
purlwise with yarn at back (WS) of work, *P4,
slip next st purlwise with yarn at back (WS)
of work, rep from * to last 3 (1: 5: 3: 2: 2) sts,
P3 (1: 5: 3: 2: 2).
Row 2: K3 (1: 5: 3: 2: 2), P1, *K4, P1, rep from
* to last 3 (1: 5: 3: 2: 2) sts, K3 (1: 5: 3: 2: 2).
These 2 rows form patt.
Cont in patt for a further 13 rows, ending with
a **RS** row.
Shape darts
Counting in from both ends of last row, place
markers on 9th (7th: 11th: 9th: 13th: 13th)
st, (miss next 9 sts and place marker on next
st) twice. There will be 6 markers in total (3
at each side) and 49 (59: 59: 69: 69: 79) sts
between markers at centre of row.
Next row (dec) (WS): (Patt to within 2 sts of
marked st, K2tog, P marked st) 3 times, (patt
to marked st, P marked st, K2tog tbl) 3 times,
patt to end.
101 (107: 115: 121: 129: 139) sts.
Work 13 rows.
Rep last 14 rows once more, then first of these
rows (the dec row) again. 89 (95: 103: 109:
117: 127) sts.
Cont straight until front measures 21 (21: 22:
22: 22: 22) cm, ending with a **RS** row.
Next row (inc) (WS): (Patt to marked st, P
marked st, M1) 3 times, (patt to marked st,
M1, P marked st) 3 times, patt to end.
Work 19 rows.
Rep last 20 rows once more, then first of these
rows (the inc row) again.
107 (113: 121: 127: 135: 145) sts.
Cont straight until front measures 37 (37: 38:
38: 38: 38) cm, ending with a WS row.

Shape armholes
Keeping patt correct, cast off 6 (7: 7: 8: 8: 9)
sts at beg of next 2 rows.
95 (99: 107: 111: 119: 127) sts.**
Dec 1 st at each end of next 5 (5: 7: 7: 9: 9)
rows, then on foll 3 (4: 5: 5: 6: 8) alt rows,
then on 2 foll 4th rows.
75 (77: 79: 83: 85: 89) sts.
Cont straight until armhole measures 16 (17:
17: 18: 19: 20) cm, ending with a WS row.
Shape front neck
Next row (RS): Patt 11 (11: 12: 13: 14: 16)
sts and turn, leaving rem sts on a holder.
Work each side of neck separately.
Keeping patt correct, dec 1 st at neck edge
of next 4 rows, then on foll alt row.
6 (6: 7: 8: 9: 11) sts.
Work 1 row, ending with a WS row.
Shape shoulder
Cast off 2 (2: 3: 3: 4: 5) sts at beg and dec
1 st at end of next row.
Work 1 row.
Cast off rem 3 (3: 3: 4: 4: 5) sts.
With RS facing, rejoin yarn to rem sts,
cast off centre 53 (55: 55: 57: 57: 57) sts,
patt to end.
Complete to match first side, reversing
shapings.

BACK
Work as given for front to **.
Dec 1 st at each end of next 2 (2: 4: 4: 6: 6)
rows, ending with a WS row.
91 (95: 99: 103: 107: 115) sts.
Place marker on centre st of last row.
Next row (RS): Work 2 tog, patt to within
4 sts of marked centre st, K4, patt marked
centre st, K4, patt to last 2 sts, work 2 tog.
Rep last row twice more.
85 (89: 93: 97: 101: 109) sts.
Next row (WS): Patt to within 4 sts of
marked centre st, K4, patt marked centre
st, K4, patt to end.
Divide for back opening
Next row (RS): Work 2 tog, patt to within
4 sts of marked centre st, K4 and turn,
leaving marked centre st and rem 42 (44: 46:
48: 50: 54) sts on a holder.
Work each side of neck separately.
Next row (WS): K4, patt to end.

Next row: Work 2 tog, patt to last 4 sts, K4.
40 (42: 44: 46: 48: 52) sts.
Last 2 rows set the sts - back opening edge
4 sts in g st with all other sts still in patt.
Keeping sts correct as now set, dec 1 st at
armhole edge of 2nd and 0 (1: 2: 2: 3: 5) alt
rows, then on 2 foll 4th rows.
37 (38: 39: 41: 42: 44) sts.
Cont straight until armhole measures 16 (17:
17: 18: 19: 20) cm, ending with a WS row.
Shape back neck
Next row (RS): Patt 11 (11: 12: 13: 14: 16)
sts, cast off rem 26 (27: 27: 28: 28: 28) sts.
Break yarn.
Rejoin yarn to rem 11 (11: 12: 13: 14: 16) sts
with WS facing and cont as folls:
Keeping patt correct, dec 1 st at neck edge of next
4 rows, then on foll alt row. 6 (6: 7: 8: 9: 11) sts.
Work 1 row, ending with a **WS** row.
Shape shoulder
Cast off 2 (2: 3: 3: 4: 5) sts at beg and dec
1 st at end of next row.
Work 1 row.
Cast off rem 3 (3: 3: 4: 4: 5) sts.
With RS facing, rejoin yarn to rem sts, K2tog,
K3, patt to last 2 sts, work 2 tog.
Next row (WS): Patt to last 4 sts, K4.
Next row: K4, patt to last 2 sts, work 2 tog.
40 (42: 44: 46: 48: 52) sts.
Last 2 rows set the sts - back opening edge
4 sts in g st with all other sts still in patt.
Complete to match first side, reversing
shapings and working first row of back neck
shaping as folls:
Shape back neck
Next row (RS): Cast off 26 (27: 27: 28: 28: 28)
sts, patt to end. 11 (11: 12: 13: 14: 16) sts.

MAKING UP
Press all pieces with a warm iron over a damp
cloth.
Join both shoulder seams using back stitch
or mattress stitch if preferred.
Neckband
With RS facing and using 2¾mm (US 2)
needles, starting and ending at back opening
edges, pick up and knit 26 (27: 27: 28: 28: 28)
from left back neck edge, 8 sts up left side of
back neck, 8 sts down left side of front neck,
53 (55: 55: 57: 57: 57) sts from front, 8 sts up
right side of front neck, 8 sts down right side
of back neck, then 26 (27: 27: 28: 28: 28)
from right back neck edge. 137 (141: 141:
145: 145: 145) sts.
Starting with a K row, work in rev st st for 4
rows, ending with a **RS** row.
Cast off knitwise (on **WS**).

Armhole borders (both alike)
With RS facing and using 2¾mm (US 2)
needles, pick up and knit 96 (104: 104: 112:
118: 124) sts evenly all round armhole edge.
Starting with a K row, work in rev st st for 4
rows, ending with a **RS** row.
Cast off knitwise (on **WS**).
Join side and armhole border seams. Make
button loop at one end of neckband and
attach button at other end to fasten back neck
opening.

55 (56: 57: 58: 59: 60) cm
21½ (22: 22½: 23: 23¼: 23¾) in

39 (41.5: 44: 46.5: 49: 53) cm
15½ (16¼: 17½: 18¼: 20¼: 21) in

SPICE
Raglan T-shirt with side vents

Recommendation
Suitable for the novice knitter
Please see pages 22 & 23 for photographs.

	XS	S	M	L	XL	XXL	
To fit	**81**	**86**	**91**	**97**	**102**	**109**	cm
bust	32	34	36	38	40	43	in

Rowan Creative Linen
3	3	4	4	5	5 x 100gm

Photographed in Coleus

Needles
1 pair 4mm (no 8) (US 6) needles
1 pair 4½mm (no 7) (US 7) needles
1 pair 5mm (no 6) (US 8) needles

Tension
18 sts and 24 rows to 10 cm measured over stocking stitch using 5mm (US 8) needles.

BACK
Cast on 77 (81: 85: 91: 95: 101) sts using 4½mm (US 7) needles.
Rows 1 and 2: P1, *K1, P1, rep from * to end.
Rows 3 and 4: K1, *P1, K1, rep from * to end.
These 4 rows form patt.
Cont in patt for a further 24 rows, ending with a WS row.
Place a marker at each end of last row.
Change to 5mm (US 8) needles.
Starting with a K row, now work in st st until back measures 37 (37: 38: 38: 38: 38) cm, ending with a WS row.
Shape raglan armholes
Cast off 4 sts at beg of next 2 rows.
69 (73: 77: 83: 87: 93) sts.
Work 2 rows.
Next row (RS): K1, K2tog, K to last 3 sts, K2tog tbl, K1.
Working all raglan armhole decreases as set by last row, dec 1 st at each end of 4th (4th: 4th: 4th: 4th: 2nd) and 4 (4: 2: 1: 0: 0) foll 4th rows, then on foll 2 (3: 7: 10: 13: 16) alt rows.
53 (55: 55: 57: 57: 57) sts.
Work 1 row, ending with a WS row.
Cast off.

FRONT
Work as given for back until 63 (65: 69: 73: 73: 73) sts rem in raglan armhole shaping.
Work 3 (1: 1: 1: 1: 1) rows, ending with a WS row.
Shape front neck
Next row (RS): (K1, K2tog) 1 (0: 1: 1: 1: 1) times, K7 (10: 9: 11: 11: 11) and turn, leaving rem sts on a holder. 9 (10: 11: 13: 13: 13) sts.
Work each side of neck separately.
Dec 1 st at neck edge of next 4 rows, then on foll 1 (1: 1: 2: 2: 2) alt rows **and at same time** dec 1 st a raglan armhole edge of 4th (2nd: 2nd: 2nd: 2nd: 2nd) and 0 (1: 2: 3: 3: 3) foll 0 (4th: alt: alt: alt: alt) rows. 3 sts.
Work 1 row, ending with a WS row.
Next row (RS): sl 1, K2tog, psso.
Work 1 row.
Fasten off.
With RS facing, rejoin yarn to rem sts, cast off centre 43 (45: 45: 45: 45: 45) sts, K to last 3 (0: 3: 3: 3: 3) sts, (K2tog tbl, K1) 1 (0: 1: 1: 1: 1) times. 9 (10: 11: 13: 13: 13) sts.
Complete to match first side, reversing shapings.

SLEEVES (both alike)
Cast on 53 (55: 55: 57: 59: 63) sts using 4½mm (US 7) needles.
Starting with a K row, work in st st as folls:
Work 6 rows, ending with a WS row.
Change to 5mm (US 8) needles.
Work 14 rows, ending with a WS row.
Shape raglan
Cast off 4 sts at beg of next 2 rows.
45 (47: 47: 49: 51: 55) sts.
Work 2 rows, ending with a WS row.
Working all raglan decreases in same way as raglan armhole decreases, dec 1 st at each end of next and 5 (5: 5: 6: 6: 6) foll 4th rows, then on foll 0 (0: 0: 0: 1: 3) alt rows.
33 (35: 35: 35: 35: 35) sts.
Work 1 (3: 3: 1: 1: 1) rows, ending with a WS row.
Left sleeve only
Dec 0 (1: 1: 1: 1: 1) st at each end of next row, then cast off 10 sts at beg of foll row. 23 sts.
Dec 1 st at beg of next row, then cast off 11 sts at beg of foll row.
Right sleeve only
Cast off 10 (11: 11: 11: 11: 11) sts at beg and dec 0 (1: 1: 1: 1: 1) st at end of next row. 23 sts.
Work 1 row.
Cast off 11 sts at beg and dec 1 st at end of next row. Work 1 row.
Both sleeves
Cast off rem 11 sts.

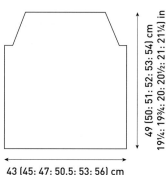

49 (50: 51: 52: 53: 54) cm
19½ (19¾: 19¾: 20: 20½: 21: 21¼) in

43 (45: 47: 50.5: 53: 56) cm
17 (17 ¾: 18 ½: 20: 21: 22) in

6cm
2 ½ in

Continued on next page...

COPPER

Striped tabard style poncho

Recommendation

Suitable for the novice knitter
Please see pages 34 & 35 for photographs.

	XS	S	M	L	XL	XXL	
To fit	**81**	**86**	**91**	**97**	**102**	**109**	**cm**
bust	32	34	36	38	40	43	in

Rowan Pima Cotton DK

A Fig							
	2	2	3	3	3	3	x 50gm
B Clay							
	1	1	2	2	2	2	x 50gm
C Leaf							
	8	8	8	9	9	10	x 50gm

Needles

1 pair 3mm (no 11) (US 2/3) needles
1 pair 3¼mm (no 10) (US 3) needles
1 pair 3¾mm (no 9) (US 5) needles

Tension

23 sts and 30 rows to 10 cm measured over
stocking stitch using 3¾mm (US 5) needles.

BACK

Cast on 131 (137: 143: 149: 155: 165) sts
using 3¼mm (US 3) needles and yarn A.
Row 1 (RS): K11, P1, *K1, P1, rep from * to
last 11 sts, K11.
Row 2: K13, P1, *K1, P1, rep from * to last
13 sts, K13.
Row 3: K11, P2, *K1, P1, rep from * to last
12 sts, P1, K11.
Row 4: K12, P1, *K1, P1, rep from * to last
12 sts, K12.
Rep last 4 rows 4 times more, then rows
1 and 2 again, ending with a WS row.
Change to 3¾mm (US 5) needles.
Row 23 (RS): K11, P1, K to last 12 sts, P1, K11.
Row 24: K12, P to last 12 sts, K12.
Last 2 rows form patt.
Cont in patt for a further 22 rows, ending
with a WS row.
Break off yarn A and join in yarn B.
Work 22 rows.
Break off yarn B and join in yarn C.
Using yarn C only, complete back as folls:
Cont in patt until back measures 27 (27: 28:
28: 28: 28) cm, ending with a **RS** row.
Shape belt openings
Place markers on 12th st in from both ends
of last row to denote base of "side" seam.
Next row: Patt 33 sts, K7, patt 51 (57: 63:
69: 75: 85) sts, K7, patt 33 sts.
Rep last row 3 times more, ending with a **RS** row.
Next row (WS): Patt 33 sts, K2, K2tog and
turn, leaving rem sts on a holder.

Work on this set of 36 sts only for first side
of back as folls:
Next row (RS): K3, patt to end.
Next row: Patt to last 3 sts, K3.
Rep last 2 rows 10 times more, ending with
a **WS** row.
Break yarn and leave these 36 sts on a 2nd holder.
With WS facing, rejoin yarn to rem sts on first
holder, K3, P51 (57: 63: 69: 75: 85), K3 and
turn, leaving rem 37 sts on holder.
Work on this set of 57 (63: 69: 75: 81: 91) sts
only for centre section as folls:
Next row (RS): Knit.
Next row: K3, P to last 3 sts, K3.
Rep last 2 rows 10 times more, ending with a
WS row.
Break yarn and leave these 57 (63: 69: 75:
81: 91) sts on a 3rd holder.
With **WS** facing, rejoin yarn to rem sts on first
holder, K2tog tbl, K2, patt to end.
Work on this set of 36 sts only for 2nd side
of back as folls:
Next row (RS): Patt to last 3 sts, K3.
Next row: K3, patt to end.
Rep last 2 rows 10 times more, ending with
a WS row.
Join sections
Next row (RS): Patt to last st of 2nd side
section, inc in last st, now patt across first
56 (62: 68: 74: 80: 90) sts of centre section
on 3rd holder, inc in last st of this section,
then patt across 36 sts on 2nd holder.
131 (137: 143: 149: 155: 165) sts.

Continued on next page...

SPICE – *Continued from previous page.*

MAKING UP

Press all pieces with a warm iron over
a damp cloth.
Join both front and right back raglan seams
using back stitch or mattress stitch if preferred.
Neckband
With RS facing and using 4mm (US 6) needles,
pick up and knit 32 sts from top of left sleeve,

8 (8: 8: 10: 10: 10) sts down left side of neck,
43 (45: 45: 45: 45: 45) sts from front,
8 (8: 8: 10: 10: 10) sts up right side of neck,
32 sts from top of right sleeve, then
52 (54: 54: 56: 56: 56) sts from back.
175 (179: 179: 185: 185: 185) sts.
Starting with a P row, work in st st for 15 rows,
ending with a WS row.

Cast off.
Join left back raglan and neckband seam,
reversing neckband seam for last 8 rows
(for rolled edge).
Join side seams from markers. Join sleeve
seams, reversing sleeve seams for first 4 cm.
Fold 3 cm cuff to RS and secure in place at
underarm.

Next row: Patt 33 sts, K7, patt 51 (57: 63: 69: 75: 85) sts, K7, patt 33 sts.
Rep last row twice more, ending with a WS row.
Place markers on 12th st in from both ends of last row to denote top of "side" seam. Belt openings are now complete.
Working all sts in patt, cont straight until back measures 66 (67: 68: 69: 70: 71) cm, ending with a WS row.

Shape shoulders
Cast off 6 (7: 7: 8: 8: 9) sts at beg of next 2 (6: 2: 6: 2: 2) rows, then 7 (0: 8: 0: 9: 10) sts at beg of foll 4 (0: 4: 0: 4: 4) rows. 91 (95: 97: 101: 103: 107) sts.

Shape back neck
Next row (RS): Cast off 7 (7: 8: 8: 9: 10) sts, K until there are 11 (12: 12: 13: 13: 14) sts on right needle and turn, leaving rem sts on a holder.
Work each side of neck separately.
Cast off 4 sts at beg of next row.
Cast off rem 7 (8: 8: 9: 9: 10) sts.
With RS facing, rejoin yarn to rem sts, cast off centre 55 (57: 57: 59: 59: 59) sts, K to end.
Complete to match first side, reversing shapings.

FRONT
Work as given for back until 2 rows less have been worked than on back to start of shoulder shaping, ending with a WS row.

Shape front neck
Next row (RS): Patt 39 (41: 44: 46: 49: 54) sts and turn, leaving rem sts on a holder.
Work each side of neck separately.
Keeping patt correct, dec 1 st at neck edge of next row. 38 (40: 43: 45: 48: 53) sts.

Shape shoulder
Cast off 6 (7: 7: 8: 8: 9) sts at beg of next and foll 0 (3: 0: 3: 0: 0) alt rows, then 7 (0: 8: 0: 9: 10) sts at beg of foll 3 (0: 3: 0: 3: 3) alt rows **and at same time** dec 1 st at neck edge of next 3 rows, then on foll alt row.
Work 1 row.
Cast off rem 7 (8: 8: 9: 9: 10) sts.
With RS facing, rejoin yarn to rem sts, cast off centre 53 (55: 55: 57: 57: 57) sts, patt to end.
Complete to match first side, reversing shapings.

MAKING UP
Press all pieces with a warm iron over a damp cloth.
Join right shoulder seam using back stitch or mattress stitch if preferred.

Neckband
With RS facing, using 3mm (US 2/3) needles and yarn C, pick up and knit 10 sts down left side of neck, 53 (55: 55: 57: 57: 57) sts from front, 10 sts up right side of neck, then 63 (65: 65: 67: 67: 67) from back.
136 (140: 140: 144: 144: 144) sts.
Starting with a K row, work in rev st st for 4 rows, ending with a **RS** row.
Cast off knitwise (on **WS**).
Join left shoulder and neckband seam. Lay front onto back with WS together and join "side" seams by stitching through both layers between markers.

Belt
Cast on 18 sts using 3mm (US 2/3) needles and yarn C.
Work in g st until belt measures 155 (160: 165: 170: 175: 180) cm.
Cast off.
Thread belt through openings in front and back as in photograph and tie at front.

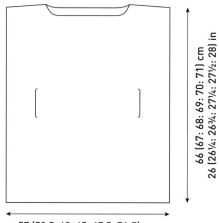

66 (67: 68: 69: 70: 71) cm
26 (26¼: 26¾: 27¼: 27½: 28) in

57 (59.5: 62: 65: 67.5: 71.5) cm
22½ (23½: 24½: 25½: 28) in

CERULEAN
Voluminous sweater with longer back

Recommendation
Suitable for the novice knitter
Please see pages 40 & 41 for photographs.

	XS	S	M	L	XL	XXL	
To fit	**81**	**86**	**91**	**97**	**102**	**109**	cm
bust	32	34	36	38	40	43	in

Rowan Panama
9	10	10	11	11	12	x 50gm

Photographed in Nightshade

Needles
1 pair 2¾mm (no 12) (US 2) needles
1 pair 3¼mm (no 10) (US 3) needles

Tension
27 sts and 36 rows to 10 cm measured over stocking stitch using 3¼mm (US 3) needles.

Pattern note: When casting off sts, slip the first st, rather than knitting it, so that the shaped shoulder edge is a smoother edge without jagged "steps".

BACK
Cast on 170 (176: 182: 190: 196: 208) sts using 2¾mm (US 2) needles.
Work in g st for 8 rows, ending with a WS row.
Change to 3¼mm (US 3) needles.
Row 9 (RS): Knit.
Row 10: K4, P to last 4 sts, K4.
Rep last 2 rows 22 times more, ending with a WS row. (For front, rep last 2 rows 13 times more so that front is 18 rows shorter than back.)
Place blue markers at both ends of last row to denote top of side seam openings.
Starting with a K row, work in st st until back measures 23 (23: 24: 24: 24: 24) cm **from blue markers,** ending with a WS row.
Shape armholes
Place red markers at both ends of last row to denote base of armholes.
Next row (RS): K3, M1, K to last 3 sts, M1, K3.
Working all armhole increases as set by last row, inc 1 st at each end of 8th (8th: 8th: 10th: 10th: 10th) and 2 (0: 0: 0: 0: 0) foll 8th rows, then on 2 (4: 4: 4: 3: 1) foll 10th rows, then on 0 (0: 0: 0: 1: 3) foll 12th rows.
182 (188: 194: 202: 208: 220) sts.**
Work 13 (13: 13: 15: 15: 15) rows, ending with a WS row.
(Armhole should measure 16 (17: 17: 18: 19: 20) cm from red markers.)
Shape shoulders
Cast off 4 (4: 4: 4: 5: 5) sts at beg of next 8 (8: 8: 4: 8: 8) rows, then 0 (0: 0: 5: 0: 0) sts at beg of foll 0 (0: 0: 4: 0: 0) rows, ending with a WS row. 150 (156: 162: 166: 168: 180) sts.
Shape back neck
Next row (RS): Cast off 4 (4: 4: 5: 5: 5) sts, K until there are 51 (53: 56: 56: 57: 63) sts on right needle and turn, leaving rem sts on a holder.
Work each side of neck separately.
Dec 1 st at neck edge of next 6 rows, then on foll 5 alt rows **and at same time** cast off 4 (4: 5: 5: 5: 5) sts at beg of 2nd and foll 4 (2: 7: 7: 7: 1) alt rows, then 5 (5: 0: 0: 0: 6) sts at beg of foll 3 (5: 0: 0: 0: 6) alt rows.
Work 1 row, ending with a WS row.
Cast off rem 5 (5: 5: 5: 6: 6) sts.
With RS facing, rejoin yarn to rem sts, cast off centre 40 (42: 42: 44: 44: 44) sts, K to end.
Complete to match first side, reversing shapings.

FRONT
Work as given for back, **noting the bracketed exception** (so front is 18 rows shorter than back), to **.
Work 3 rows, ending with a WS row.
Shape front neck
Next row (RS): K74 (76: 79: 83: 86: 92) and turn, leaving rem sts on a holder.
Work each side of neck separately.
Dec 1 st at neck edge of next 6 rows, then on foll 1 (1: 1: 2: 2: 2) alt rows.
67 (69: 72: 75: 78: 84) sts.
Work 1 row, ending with a WS row.
Shape shoulder
Cast off 4 (4: 4: 4: 5: 5) sts at beg of next and foll 9 (7: 4: 1: 12: 6) alt rows, then 5 (5: 5: 5: 0: 6) sts at beg of foll 3 (5: 8: 11: 0: 6) alt rows **and at same time** dec 1 st at neck edge of next and foll 2 alt rows, then on 4 foll 4th rows.
Work 1 row, ending with a WS row.
Cast off rem 5 (5: 5: 5: 6: 6) sts.
With RS facing, rejoin yarn to rem sts, cast off centre 34 (36: 36: 36: 36: 36) sts, K to end.
Complete to match first side, reversing shapings.

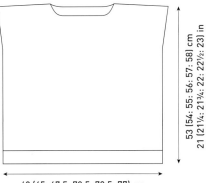

63 (65: 67.5: 70.5: 72.5: 77) cm
24¾ (25½: 26½: 27½: 28½: 30¼) in

53 (54: 55: 56: 57: 58) cm
21 (21¼: 21¾: 22: 22½: 23) in

9 cm
3½ in

Continued on next page...

PLENTY
Classic raglan sweater with short sleeves

Recommendation
Suitable for the knitter with a little experience
Please see page 7 for photograph.

	XS	S	M	L	XL	XXL	
To fit	**81**	**86**	**91**	**97**	**102**	**109**	**cm**
bust	32	34	36	38	40	43	in

Rowan Kidsilk Haze and Fine Lace
A Kidsilk Haze

        3   3   3   4   4   5 x 25gm

B Fine Lace

        2   2   2   2   2   3 x 50gm

Photographed in Kidsilk Haze in Turkish Plum
and Fine Lace in Aged

Needles
1 pair 3mm (no 11) (US 2/3) needles
1 pair 3¼mm (no 10) (US 3) needles

Tension
23 sts and 31 rows to 10 cm measured over
stocking stitch using 3¼mm (US 3) needles and
one strand each of yarns A and B held together.

Special note:
We found it preferable to knit the two yarns
together from separate balls rather than
winding them together.

BACK
Cast on 94 (98: 106: 110: 118: 126) sts
loosely using 3mm (US 2/3) needles and
one strand each of yarns A and B held
together.
Row 1 (RS): K2, *P2, K2, rep from * to end.
Row 2: P2, *K2, P2, rep from * to end.
These 2 rows form rib.
Cont in rib until back measures 7 cm, dec
1 (0: 1: 0: 1: 1) st at each end of last row
and ending with a WS row.
92 (98: 104: 110: 116: 124) sts.
Change to 3¼mm (US 3) needles.
Starting with a K row, now work in st st until
back measures 38 (38: 39: 39: 39: 39) cm,
ending with a WS row.
Shape raglan armholes
Cast off 5 sts at beg of next 2 rows.
82 (88: 94: 100: 106: 114) sts.
Work 2 (2: 0: 0: 0: 0) rows.
Next row (RS): K1, K2tog, K to last 3 sts,
K2tog tbl, K1.
Next row: (P1, P2tog tbl) 0 (0: 0: 0: 1: 1)
times, P to last 0 (0: 0: 0: 3: 3) sts, (P2tog,
P1) 0 (0: 0: 0: 1: 1) times.
80 (86: 92: 98: 102: 110) sts.
Working all raglan armhole decreases
as set by last 2 rows, cont as folls:

Dec 1 st at each end of 3rd (3rd: next: next:
next: next) row and foll 0 (0: 0: 0: 2: 6) rows,
then on 1 (1: 0: 0: 0: 0) foll 4th row, then
on foll 8 (10: 14: 16: 16: 16) alt rows.
60 (62: 62: 64: 64: 64) sts.
Work 1 row, ending with a WS row.
Cast off **loosely**.

FRONT
Work as given for back until 72 (74: 74:
78: 78: 78) sts rem in raglan armhole
shaping.
Work 1 row, ending with a WS row.
Shape front neck
Next row (RS): K1, K2tog, K9 (9: 9: 12: 12:
12) and turn, leaving rem sts on a holder.
11 (11: 11: 14: 14: 14) sts.
Work each side of neck separately.
Dec 1 st at neck edge of next 5 (5: 5: 7:
7: 7) rows, ending with a WS row, **and at
same time** dec 1 st at raglan armhole
edge of 2nd and foll 1 (1: 1: 2: 2: 2)
alt rows. 4 sts.
Next row (RS): K1, K3tog.
Work 1 row.
Next row: K2tog and fasten off.
With RS facing, rejoin yarns to rem
sts, cast off centre 48 (50: 50: 48:
48: 48) sts **loosely**, K to last 3 sts,
K2tog tbl, K1.
11 (11: 11: 14: 14: 14) sts.
Complete to match first side, reversing
shapings.

CERULEAN – *Continued from previous page.*

SLEEVES (both alike)
Cast on 86 (92: 92: 96: 102: 108) sts using
2¾mm (US 2) needles.
Starting with a K row, now work in st st as folls:
Work 6 rows.
Change to 3¼mm (US 3) needles.
Work 30 rows, ending with a WS row.
Cast off.

MAKING UP
Press all pieces with a warm iron over a damp cloth.

Join right shoulder seam using back stitch
or mattress stitch if preferred.
Neckband
With RS facing and using 2¾mm (US 2)
needles, pick up and knit 30 (30: 30: 32: 32:
32) down left side of front neck, 34 (36: 36:
36: 36: 36) sts from front, 30 (30: 30: 32: 32:
32) sts up right side of front neck, 17 sts down
right side of back neck, 40 (42: 42: 44: 44:
44) from back, then 17 sts up left side of back
neck. 168 (172: 172: 178: 178: 178) sts.

Starting with a K row, work in rev st st
for 6 rows, ending with a **RS** row.
Cast off knitwise (on **WS**).
Join left shoulder and neckband seam.
Sew cast-off edge of sleeves to back and
front between red markers.
Join side and sleeve seams, leaving side
seams open below blue markers and
reversing sleeve seam for first 8 rows.
Allow first 6 rows of sleeve to roll to RS
and secure in place at sleeve seam.

SLEEVES (both alike)

Cast on 62 (62: 66: 66: 70: 70) sts **loosely** using 3mm (US 2/3) needles and one strand each of yarns A and B held together.
Work in rib as given for back for 3 cm, inc 0 (1: 0: 1: 0: 1) st at each end of last row and ending with a WS row.
62 (64: 66: 68: 70: 72) sts.
Change to 3¼mm (US 3) needles.
Starting with a K row, work in st st as folls:
Work 2 rows, ending with a WS row.

Next row (RS): K3, M1, K to last 3 sts, M1, K3.
64 (66: 68: 70: 72: 74) sts.
Work 3 rows, ending with a WS row.

Shape raglan

Cast off 5 sts at beg of next 2 rows.
54 (56: 58: 60: 62: 64) sts.
Work 2 rows, ending with a WS row.
Working all raglan decreases in same way as raglan armhole decreases, dec 1 st at each end of next and 4 (5: 4: 5: 5: 6) foll 4th rows, then on foll 2 (2: 4: 4: 5: 5) alt rows. 40 sts.
Work 1 row, ending with a WS row.

Left sleeve only

Dec 1 st at each end of next row, then cast off 11 sts at beg of foll row. 27 sts.
Dec 1 st at beg of next row, then cast off 13 sts at beg of foll row.

Right sleeve only

Cast off 12 sts at beg and dec 1 st at end of next row. 27 sts.
Work 1 row.
Cast off 13 sts at beg and dec 1 st at end of next row.
Work 1 row.

Both sleeves

Cast off rem 13 sts.

MAKING UP

Press all pieces with a warm iron over a damp cloth.
Join both front and right back raglan seams using back stitch or mattress stitch if preferred.

Neckband

With RS facing, using 3mm (US 2/3) needles and one strand each of yarns A and B held together, pick up and knit 36 sts from top of left sleeve placing a marker between centre 2 sts, 7 (7: 7: 9: 9: 9) sts down left side of neck, 48 (50: 50: 48: 48: 48) sts from front, 7 (7: 7: 9: 9: 9) sts up right side of neck, 36 sts from top of right sleeve placing a marker between centre 2 sts, then 58 (60: 60: 62: 62: 62) sts from front.
192 (196: 196: 200: 200: 200) sts.

Rows 1 to 3: Knit.
Row 4 (RS): *K to within 4 sts of marker, K2tog, K4 (marker is between centre 2 sts of these 4 sts), K2tog tbl, rep from * once more, K to end.
Rep last 4 rows 3 times more, ending with a RS row.
Cast off rem 176 (180: 180: 184: 184: 184) sts knitwise (on **WS**).
Join left back raglan and neckband seam.
Join side and sleeve seams.

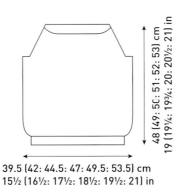

48 (49: 50: 51: 52: 53) cm
19 (19¼: 19¾: 20: 20½: 21) in

39.5 (42: 44.5: 47: 49.5: 53.5) cm
15½ (16½: 17½: 18½: 19½: 21) in

5cm
2 in

SIZZLE

Pretty top with internal shaping

Recommendation

Suitable for the knitter with a little experience
Please see pages 26 & 27 for photographs.

	XS	S	M	L	XL	XXL	
To fit	**81**	**86**	**91**	**97**	**102**	**109**	cm
bust	32	34	36	38	40	43	in

Rowan Pima Cotton DK

| | 6 | 6 | 7 | 7 | 8 | 9 | x 50gm |

Photographed in Maple

Needles

1 pair 3mm (no 11) (US 2/3) needles
1 pair 3¼mm (no 10) (US 3) needles

Buttons – 7

Tension

26 sts and 34 rows to 10 cm measured over
stocking stitch using 3¼mm (US 3) needles.

BACK

Cast on 105 (111: 117: 125: 131: 141) sts
using 3mm (US 2/3) needles.
Row 1 (RS): P1, *K1, P1, rep from * to end.
Row 2: As row 1.
Rows 3 and 4: K1, *P1, K1, rep from * to end.
These 4 rows form double moss st.
Work in double moss st for a further 8 rows,
ending with a WS row.
Change to 3¼mm (US 3) needles.
Starting with a K row, now work in st st as folls:
Work 6 rows, ending with a WS row.
Next row (dec) (RS): K9, K2tog tbl, K to last
11 sts, K2tog, K9.
Working all side seam decreases as set by last
row, dec 1 st at each end of 6th and 2 foll 6th
rows, then on 5 foll 4th rows.
87 (93: 99: 107: 113: 123) sts.
Work 15 rows, ending with a WS row.
Next row (inc) (RS): K3, M1, K to last 3 sts, M1, K3.
Working all side seam increases as set by last
row, inc 1 st at each end of 6th and 5 foll 6th
rows, then on 2 foll 8th rows.
105 (111: 117: 125: 131: 141) sts.
Cont straight until back measures 40 (40: 41:
41: 41: 41) cm, ending with a WS row.
Shape raglan armholes
Cast off 5 sts at beg of next 2 rows.
95 (101: 107: 115: 121: 131) sts.
Work 2 (2: 2: 2: 2: 0) rows.
Next row (RS): K1, K2tog, K to last 3 sts,
K2tog tbl, K1.
Next row: (P1, P2tog tbl) 0 (0: 0: 0: 0: 1)
times, P to last 0 (0: 0: 0: 0: 3) sts, (P2tog, P1)
0 (0: 0: 0: 0: 1) times.
93 (99: 105: 113: 119: 127) sts.
Working all raglan armhole decreases as set
by last 2 rows, cont as folls:
Dec 1 st at each end of 3rd (3rd: 3rd: 3rd:
next: next) row and foll 0 (0: 0: 0: 0: 2) rows,
then on 5 (5: 2: 1: 0: 0) foll 4th rows, then
on foll 2 (4: 10: 14: 18: 20) alt rows.
77 (79: 79: 81: 81: 81) sts.
Work 1 row, ending with a WS row.
Cast of rem sts.

Pattern note: Row-end edges of fronts forms
actual front opening edges. To ensure edges
remains neat and tidy, make sure new balls of
yarn are joined in at side seam edges **only**.

LEFT FRONT

Cast on 59 (62: 65: 69: 72: 77) sts using
3mm (US 2/3) needles.
Row 1 (RS): *P1, K1, rep from * to last
1 (0: 1: 1: 0: 1) st, P1 (0: 1: 1: 0: 1).
Row 2: P1 (0: 1: 1: 0: 1), *K1, P1, rep from
* to end.
Row 3: *K1, P1, rep from * to last 1 (0: 1:
0: 1) st, K1 (0: 1: 1: 0: 1).
Row 4: K1 (0: 1: 1: 0: 1), *P1, K1, rep from
* to end.
These 4 rows form double moss st.
Work in double moss st for a further 8 rows,
ending with a WS row.
Change to 3¼mm (US 3) needles.
Row 13 (RS): K to last 8 sts, patt 8 sts.
Row 14: Patt 8 sts, P to end.
Last 2 rows set the sts - front opening edge
8 sts still in double moss st with all other sts
now in st st.
Keeping sts correct as now set, cont as folls:
Work 4 rows, ending with a WS row.
Working all side seam decreases in same way
as back side seam decreases, dec 1 st at beg
of next and 3 foll 6th rows, then on 5 foll 4th
rows. 50 (53: 56: 60: 63: 68) sts.
Work 15 rows, ending with a WS row.
Working all side seam increases in same way
as back side seam increases, inc 1 st at beg
of next and 6 foll 6th rows, then on 2 foll 8th
rows. 59 (62: 65: 69: 72: 77) sts.
Cont straight until left front matches back to
start of raglan armhole shaping, ending with
a WS row.
Shape raglan armhole
Keeping sts correct, cast off 5 sts at beg of
next row. 54 (57: 60: 64: 67: 72) sts.
Work 3 (3: 3: 3: 3: 1) rows.
Working all raglan armhole decreases as set
by back, dec 1 st at raglan armhole edge of
next 1 (1: 1: 1: 1: 5) rows, then on 3 (4: 3: 2:
0: 0) foll 4th rows, then on foll 0 (0: 3: 6: 11:
12) alt rows. 50 (52: 53: 55: 55: 55) sts.
Work 3 (3: 1: 1: 1: 1) rows, ending with
a WS row.
Shape front neck
Next row (RS): K1, K2tog, K8 (9: 10: 12: 12:
12) and turn, leaving rem 39 (40: 40: 40: 40:
40) sts on a holder.
10 (11: 12: 14: 14: 14) sts.

Dec 1 st at neck edge of next 6 rows, then on foll 0 (0: 0: 1: 1: 1) alt row **and at same time** dec 1 st at raglan armhole edge on 4th (4th: 2nd: 2nd: 2nd: 2nd) and foll 0 (1: 2: 3: 3: 3) alt rows. 3 sts.

Work 1 row, ending with a WS row.

Next row (RS): K1, K2tog.

Next row: P2.

Next row: K2tog and fasten off.

Mark positions for 7 buttons along left front opening edge - first button to come level with row 9, 7th button to come 2 cm above neck shaping, and rem 5 buttons evenly spaced between.

RIGHT FRONT

Cast on 59 (62: 65: 69: 72: 77) sts using 3mm (US 2/3) needles.

Row 1 (RS): P1 (0: 1: 1: 0: 1), *K1, P1, rep from * to end.

Row 2: *P1, K1, rep from * to last 1 (0: 1: 1: 0: 1) st, P1 (0: 1: 1: 0: 1).

Row 3: K1 (0: 1: 1: 0: 1), *P1, K1, rep from * to end.

Row 4: *K1, P1, rep from * to last 1 (0: 1: 1: 0: 1) st, K1 (0: 1: 1: 0: 1).

These 4 rows form double moss st.

Work in double moss st for a further 4 rows, ending with a WS row.

Row 9 (buttonhole row) (RS): Patt 3 sts, work 2 tog tbl, yrn (to make a buttonhole), patt to end.

Working a further 5 buttonholes in this way to correspond with positions marked for buttons on left front and noting that no further reference will be made to buttonholes, cont as folls:

Work a further 3 rows, ending with a WS row.

Change to 3¼mm (US 3) needles.

Row 13 (RS): Patt 8 sts, K to end.

Row 14: P to last 8 sts, patt 8 sts.

Last 2 rows set the sts - front opening edge 8 sts still in double moss st with all other sts now in st st.

Complete to match left front, reversing shapings and working first row of neck shaping as folls:

Shape front neck

Next row (RS): Patt 39 (40: 40: 40: 40: 40) sts and slip these sts onto a holder, K to last 3 sts, K2tog tbl, K1. 10 (11: 12: 14: 14: 14) sts.

SLEEVES (both alike)

Cast on 73 (75: 75: 77: 79: 81) sts using 3mm (US 2/3) needles.

Work in double moss st as given for back for 6 rows, ending with a WS row.

Shape raglan

Keeping patt correct, cast off 5 sts at beg of next 2 rows.

63 (65: 65: 67: 69: 71) sts.

Work in double moss st for a further 4 rows, dec 1 st at each end of 3rd of these rows and ending with a WS row.

61 (63: 63: 65: 67: 69) sts.

Change to 3¼mm (US 3) needles.

Starting with a K row, now work in st st as folls: Working all raglan decreases in same way as raglan armhole decreases, dec 1 st at each end of 3rd and 5 (6: 6: 7: 7: 8) foll 4th rows, then on foll 0 (0: 0: 0: 1: 1) alt row. 49 sts.

Work 1 row, ending with a WS row.

Left sleeve only

Dec 1 st at each end of next row, then cast off 14 sts at beg of foll row. 33 sts.

Dec 1 st at beg of next row, then cast off 16 sts at beg of foll row.

Right sleeve only

Cast off 15 sts at beg and dec 1 st at end of next row. 33 sts.

Work 1 row.

Cast off 16 sts at beg and dec 1 st at end of next row.

Work 1 row.

Both sleeves

Cast off rem 16 sts.

MAKING UP

Press all pieces with a warm iron over a damp cloth.

Join all raglan seams using back stitch or mattress stitch if preferred.

Neckband

With RS facing and using 3mm (US 2/3) needles, slip 39 (40: 40: 40: 40: 40) sts on right front holder onto right needle, rejoin yarn and pick up and knit 7 (7: 7: 9: 9: 9) sts up right side of neck, one st from raglan seam (mark this st with a coloured thread), 45 sts from top of right sleeve, one st from raglan seam (mark this st with a coloured thread), 73 (75: 75: 77: 77: 77) sts from back, one st from raglan seam (mark this st with a coloured thread), 45 sts from top of left sleeve, one st from raglan seam (mark this st with a coloured thread), and 7 (7: 7: 9: 9: 9) sts down left side of neck, then patt 39 (40: 40: 40: 40: 40) sts on left front holder.

259 (263: 263: 269: 269: 269) sts.

Now place 2nd pair of markers across top of sts of each sleeve as folls: miss marked st and next 15 sts, then place marker on next st. There should now be 4 markers across top of each sleeve - 8 markers in total.

Row 1 (WS): Patt 8 sts, P to last 8 sts, patt 8 sts.

Now working all sts in double moss st as set by front opening edge sts, cont as folls:

Row 2 (RS): *Patt to within one st of marked st, work 3 tog (marked st is centre st of these 3 sts), rep from * 7 times more, patt to end.

243 (247: 247: 253: 253: 253) sts.

Work 5 rows.

Row 8: Patt 3 sts, work 2 tog tbl, yrn (to make 7th buttonhole), *patt to within one st of marked st, work 3 tog (marked st is centre st of these 3 sts), rep from * 7 times more, patt to end.

227 (231: 231: 237: 237: 237) sts.

Work 3 rows.

Row 12: As row 2.

211 (215: 215: 221: 221: 221) sts.

Cast off in patt (on **WS**).

Join side and sleeve seams. Sew on buttons.

50 [51: 52: 53: 54: 55) cm
19½ (20: 20½: 21: 21¼: 21½) in

40.5 (43: 45.5: 48: 50.5: 54.5) cm
16 (17: 18: 19: 20: 21½) in

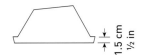

1.5 cm
½ in

HOT
Openwork raglan sweatshirt

Recommendation

Suitable for the knitter with a little experience
Please see pages 24 & 25 for photographs.

	XS	S	M	L	XL	XXL	
To fit	**81**	**86**	**91**	**97**	**102**	**109**	cm
bust	32	34	36	38	40	43	in

Rowan Creative Linen

| | 4 | 4 | 4 | 5 | 5 | 6 x 100gm |

Photographed in Coleus

Needles

1 pair 3¼mm (no 10) (US 3) needles
1 pair 4mm (no 8) (US 6) needles
1 pair 8mm (no 0) (US 11) needles

Tension

12 sts and 18 rows to 10 cm measured over
pattern using a combination of 4mm (US 6)
and 8mm (US 11) needles.

BACK and FRONT (both alike)

Cast on 102 (106: 110: 114: 118: 126) sts
using 3¼mm (US 3) needles.
Row 1 (RS): K2, *P2, K2, rep from * to end.
Row 2: P2, *K2, P2, rep from * to end.
These 2 rows form rib.
Cont in rib for a further 21 rows, ending
with a **RS** row.
Change to 4mm (US 6) needles.
Row 24 (WS): P0 (0: 1: 0: 2: 0), (P2tog)
0 (1: 0: 0: 0: 0) times, (P1, P2tog) 34 (34:
36: 38: 38: 42) times, P0 (0: 1: 0: 2: 0),
(P2tog) 0 (1: 0: 0: 0: 0) times.
68 (70: 74: 76: 80: 84) sts.
Now work in patt as folls:
Row 1 (RS): Using an 8mm (US 11) needle,
knit.
Row 2: Using a 4mm (US 6) needle, purl.
These 2 rows form patt.
Cont in patt until work measures 37 (37: 38:
38: 38: 38) cm, ending with a WS row.
Shape raglan armholes
Keeping patt correct, cast off 4 sts at beg
of next 2 rows.
60 (62: 66: 68: 72: 76) sts.
Work 2 rows.
Next row (RS): K1, K2tog, K to last 3 sts,
K2tog tbl, K1.
Working all raglan armhole decreases as set
by last row, dec 1 st at each end of 4th and
2 (3: 1: 2: 1: 0) foll 4th rows, then on foll
11 (10: 14: 13: 16: 19) alt rows.
30 (32: 32: 34: 34: 34) sts.
Work 1 row, ending with a WS row.
Using an 8mm (US 11) needle, cast off.

SLEEVES (both alike)

Cast on 42 (46: 46: 46: 50: 50) sts using
3¼mm (US 3) needles.
Work in rib as given for back and front for
23 rows, dec 0 (1: 1: 0: 1: 0) st at each end
of last row and ending with a **RS** row.
42 (44: 44: 46: 48: 50) sts.
Now work in patt as folls:
Row 1 (WS): Using a 4mm (US 6) needle,
purl.
Row 2: Using an 8mm (US 11) needle, knit.
These 2 rows form patt.
Keeping patt correct throughout, cont as folls:
Work 1 row.

Next row (RS): K3, M1, K to last 3 sts,
M1, K3.
Working all increases as set by last row, inc
1 st at each end of 4th (4th: 6th: 6th: 6th:
6th) and every foll 4th (6th: 6th: 6th: 6th:
6th) row to 48 (60: 60: 60: 60: 60) sts,
then on every foll 6th (-: -: 8th: 8th: 8th)
row until there are 58 (-: -: 62: 64: 66) sts.
Cont straight until sleeve measures 35 (36:
37: 38: 39: 40) cm, ending with a WS row.
Shape raglan
Keeping patt correct, cast off 4 sts at beg
of next 2 rows.
50 (52: 52: 54: 56: 58) sts.
Work 2 rows.

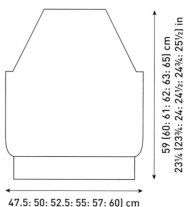

59 (60: 61: 62: 63: 65) cm
23¼ (23¾: 24: 24½: 24¾: 25½) in

47.5: 50: 52.5: 55: 57: 60) cm
18¾ (19¾: 20¾: 21½: 22½: 23½) in

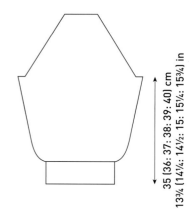

35 (36: 37: 38: 39: 40) cm
13¾ (14¼: 14½: 15: 15¼: 15¾) in

Continued on next page...

GLEAM
Crochet scarf with fringing

SCARF
Make 19 ch using 4.00mm (US G6) crochet hook.
Foundation row (RS): 1 dc into 2nd ch from hook, 1 dc into each ch to end, turn. 18 sts.
Now work in patt as folls:
Row 1 (WS): 1 ch (does NOT count as st), 1 dc into each dc to end, turn.
Row 2: As row 1.
Row 3: 5 ch (counts as first ttr), miss first dc, 1 ttr into each dc to end, turn.
Row 4: 1 ch (does NOT count as st), 1 dc into each ttr to end, working last dc into top of 5 ch at beg of previous row, turn.
These 4 rows form patt.
Cont in patt until scarf measures approx 175 cm, ending after patt row 2.
Fasten off.
Fringe
Cut 96 lengths of yarn, each 54 cm long, and knot groups of 6 of these lengths through each end of scarf, positioning 8 knots evenly along each edge.

Recommendation
Suitable for the novice crocheter
Please see page 37 for photograph.

Rowan Panama
2   x 50gm
Photographed in Begonia

Crochet hook
4.00mm (no 8) (US G6) crochet hook

Tension
18 sts to 10 cm and 3 patt reps (12 rows) to **12** cm measured over pattern using 4.00mm (US G6) crochet hook.

Finished size
Completed scarf measures 10 cm (4 ins) wide and 175 cm (69 ins) long excluding fringe.

Crochet abbreviations
ch = chain; **dc** = double crochet; **ttr** = triple treble.
See page 99 for further details.

HOT – *Continued from previous page.*

Working all raglan decreases in same way as raglan armhole decreases, dec 1 st at each end of next and 2 foll 4th rows, then on every foll alt row until 18 sts rem.
Work 1 row, ending with a WS row.
Using an 8mm (US 11) needle, cast off.

MAKING UP
Press all pieces with a warm iron over a damp cloth.

Join both front and right back raglan seams using back stitch or mattress stitch if preferred.
Neckband
With RS facing and using 3¼mm (US 3) needles, pick up and knit 24 sts from top of left sleeve, 43 (45: 45: 47: 47: 47) sts from front, 24 sts from top of right sleeve, then 43 (45: 45: 47: 47: 47) sts from back. 134 (138: 138: 142: 142: 142) sts.

Starting with row 2, work in rib as given for back and front for 6 rows, ending with a **RS** row.
Cast off in rib (on **WS**).
Join left back raglan and neckband seam.
Join side and sleeve seams.

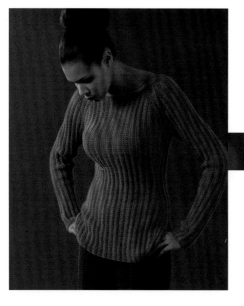

JUICY
Sculpted ribbed raglan sweater

Recommendation
Suitable for the more experienced knitter
Please see pages 32 & 33 for photographs.

	XS	S	M	L	XL	XXL	
To fit	**81**	**86**	**91**	**97**	**102**	**109**	cm
bust	32	34	36	38	40	43	in

Rowan Handknit Cotton
| 12 | 13 | 14 | 14 | 15 | 16 x 50gm |
Photographed in Burnt

Needles
1 pair 3¼mm (no 10) (US 3) needles
1 pair 4mm (no 8) (US 6) needles

Tension
22 sts and 31 rows to 10 cm measured over
pattern using 4mm (US 6) needles.

BACK and FRONT (both alike)
Cast on 55 (63: 71: 79: 87: 95) sts using
4mm (US 6) needles.
Row 1 (RS): K1, P1, *K3, P1, rep from * to
last st, K1.
Counting in from both ends of last row, place
marker after 9th st in from ends of rows.
Row 2: (K1, P1) twice, K3, P1, K1, slip marker
onto right needle, M1, K2, *P1, K3, rep from
* to last 12 sts, P1, K2, M1, slip marker onto
right needle, K1, P1, K3, (P1, K1) twice.
These 2 rows set the sts - 9 st moss st and
patt borders with all other sts in patt.
Keeping patt correct and taking inc sts into
patt, cont as folls:
Row 3: Patt to marker, slip marker onto right
needle, M1, patt to next marker, M1, slip
marker onto right needle, patt to end.
Rows 4 and 5: As row 3.
63 (71: 79: 87: 95: 103) sts.
Row 6: Patt 9 sts, slip marker to right needle,
patt to next marker, slip marker to right needle,
patt 9 sts.
Row 7: As row 3.
Rep last 2 rows 6 times more.
77 (85: 93: 101: 109: 117) sts.
Rows 20 to 22: As row 6.
Row 23: As row 3.
Rep last 4 rows 4 times more.
87 (95: 103: 111: 119: 127) sts.
Place markers at both ends of last row
to denote top of side seam openings.
Now working **all** sts in patt, cont as folls:
Work 11 rows, ending with a WS row.
Next row (dec) (RS): Patt to marker, slip
marker onto right needle, work 2 tog, patt
to within 2 sts of next marker, work 2 tog tbl,
slip marker onto right needle, patt 9 sts.
Keeping patt correct and working all decreases
as set by last row, dec 1 st at each end of
4th and 6 foll 4th rows.
71 (79: 87: 95: 103: 111) sts.
Work 13 rows, ending with a WS row.
Next row (inc) (RS): Patt to marker, slip marker
onto right needle, M1, patt to next marker, M1,
slip marker onto right needle, patt to end.
Keeping patt correct and working all increases
as set by last row, inc 1 st at each end of 4th
and 3 foll 4th rows, then on 3 foll 6th rows.
87 (95: 103: 111: 119: 127) sts.

Cont straight until work measures 44 (44: 45:
45: 45: 45) cm, ending with a WS row.
Shape raglan armholes
Keeping patt correct, cast off 4 sts at beg
of next 2 rows.
79 (87: 95: 103: 111: 119) sts.
Work 2 (2: 2: 0: 0: 0) rows, ending with
a WS row.
Sizes XS and S only
Next row (RS): K1, P1, K3, P2tog, patt to last
7 sts, P2tog tbl, K3, P1, K1.
Next row: K3, P1, K2, patt to last 6 sts, K2,
P1, K3.
Next row: K1, P1, K3, P1, patt to last 6 sts,
P1, K3, P1, K1.
Next row: K3, P1, K2, patt to last 6 sts, K2,
P1, K3.
Rep last 4 rows 5 (3: -: -: -: -) times more.
67 (79: -: -: -: -) sts.
Sizes L, XL and XXL only
Next row (RS): K1, P1, K3, P2tog, patt to last
7 sts, P2tog tbl, K3, P1, K1.
Next row: K3, P1, K1, K2tog tbl, patt to last
7 sts, K2tog, K1, P1, K3.
Rep last 2 rows - (-: -: 0: 3: 5) times more.
- (-: -: 99: 95: 95) sts.
All sizes
Next row (RS): K1, P1, K3, P2tog, patt to
last 7 sts, P2tog tbl, K3, P1, K1.
Next row: K3, P1, K2, patt to last 6 sts, K2,
P1, K3.
Rep last 2 rows 3 (9: 17: 19: 17: 17) times
more. 59 sts.
Next row (RS): K1, P1, K3, P2tog, patt to
last 7 sts, P2tog tbl, K3, P1, K1.
Next row: K2tog, K1, P1, K2, patt to last 6 sts,
K2, P1, K1, K2tog tbl.
Break yarn and leave rem 55 sts on a holder.
Counting in from both ends of last row, place
markers after 5th st in from both ends of row.

SLEEVES (both alike)
Cast on 47 (47: 51: 51: 55: 55) sts using
4mm (US 6) needles.
Row 1 (RS): K1, P1, *K3, P1, rep from * to
last st, K1.
Row 2: K3, *P1, K3, rep from * to end.
These 2 rows form patt.
Work in patt for a further 10 rows, ending
with a WS row.

Counting in from both ends of last row, place markers after 6th st in from both ends of row.

Row 13 (RS): Patt to marker, slip marker onto right needle, M1, patt to next marker, M1, slip marker onto right needle, patt to end.
Keeping patt correct and working all increases as set by last row, inc 1 st at each end of 10th (10th: 12th: 10th: 12th: 12th) and every foll 10th (10th: 12th: 12th: 12th: 12th) row to 57 (53: 75: 75: 75: 73) sts, then on every foll 12th (12th: -: -: 14th: 14th) row until there are 71 (71: -: -: 79: 79) sts, taking inc sts into patt.
Cont straight until sleeve measures 48 (49: 50: 51: 52: 53) cm, ending with a WS row.

Shape raglan
Keeping patt correct, cast off 4 sts at beg of next 2 rows. 63 (63: 67: 67: 71: 71) sts.
Work 2 rows.
Working all raglan decreases as set by raglan armhole decreases, dec 1 st at each end of next and 3 (5: 3: 5: 4: 6) foll 4th rows, then on foll 10 (8: 12: 10: 13: 11) alt rows, ending with a **RS** row. 35 sts.
Next row (WS): K2tog, K1, P1, K2, patt to last 6 sts, K2, P1, K1, K2tog tbl.
Break yarn and leave rem 33 sts on a holder.
Counting in from both ends of last row, place markers after 5th st in from both ends of row.

MAKING UP
Press all pieces with a warm iron over a damp cloth.
Join both front and right back raglan seams using back stitch or mattress stitch if preferred.

Neckband
With RS facing and using 3¼mm (US 3) needles, work across sts of left sleeve as folls:
patt to marker, slip marker onto right needle, P2tog, patt to within 2 sts of next marker, P2tog tbl, slip marker onto right needle, patt to last st, P tog last st of left sleeve with first st of front, rep from * to * across sts of front, P tog last st of front with first st of right sleeve, rep from * to * across sts of right sleeve, P tog last st of right sleeve with first st of back, rep from * to * across sts of back, patt last st of back. 165 sts.
Keeping each section of patt correct as now set, cont as folls:
Work 1 row.
Next row (RS): *Patt to next marker, slip marker onto right needle, P2tog, patt to within 2 sts of next marker, P2tog tbl, slip marker onto right needle, rep from * 3 times more, patt to end. 157 sts.
Rep last 2 rows twice more. 141 sts.
Work 1 row, ending with a WS row.

Cast off in patt.
Join left back raglan and neckband seam. Join side and sleeve seams, leaving side seams open below side seam markers.

39.5 (43: 47: 50.5: 54: 57.5) cm
15½ (17: 18½: 20: 21¼: 22½) in

56 (57: 58: 59: 60: 61) cm
22 (22½: 23: 23¼: 23¾: 24) in

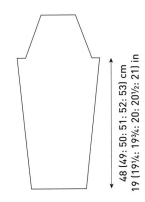

48 (49: 50: 51: 52: 53) cm
19 (19¼: 19¾: 20: 20½: 21) in

SEARING

Pretty eyelet peplum cardigan

Recommendation

Suitable for the knitter with a little experience
Please see pages 18, 19 & 21 for photographs.

	XS	S	M	L	XL	XXL	
To fit	**81**	**86**	**91**	**97**	**102**	**109**	**cm**
bust	32	34	36	38	40	43	**in**

Rowan Handknit Cotton

10 11 11 12 13 14 x 50gm
Photographed in Raspberry

Needles

1 pair 3¼mm (no 10) (US 3) needles
1 pair 4mm (no 8) (US 6) needles

Buttons – 5

Tension

20 sts and 28 rows to 10 cm measured over
pattern using 4mm (US 6) needles.

Special abbreviations

Tw2 = K into front of 2nd st on left needle
leaving sts on left needle, then K into first st on
left needle and slip both sts off left needle at
same time.

Pattern note: When working patt from charts,
twist sts between each band of lace patt are
worked on RS rows, whilst eyelet holes that
form zig zag lines of lace patt are worked on
WS rows.

BACK

Cast on 88 (92: 98: 102: 108: 116) sts using
3¼mm (US 3) needles.
Work in g st as folls:
Work 4 rows, ending with a WS row.
Row 5 (RS): K7, K2tog tbl, K to last 9 sts,
K2tog, K7.
Work 3 rows.
Rep last 4 rows 8 times more, then row 5
again. 68 (72: 78: 82: 88: 96) sts.
Work 7 rows, ending with a WS row.
Change to 4mm (US 6) needles.
Beg and ending rows as indicated and
repeating the 20 row patt rep throughout,
cont in patt from chart for back as folls:
Inc 1 st at each end of 7th and 2 foll 6th rows,
then on 4 foll 8th rows, taking inc sts into patt.
82 (86: 92: 96: 102: 110) sts.
Cont straight until back measures 33 (33: 34:
34: 34: 34) cm, ending with a WS row.
Shape armholes
Keeping patt correct, cast off 4 (4: 5: 5: 6: 6)
sts at beg of next 2 rows.
74 (78: 82: 86: 90: 98) sts.
Dec 1 st at each end of next 3 (3: 5: 5: 7: 7)
rows, then on foll 1 (2: 1: 2: 1: 3) alt rows,
then on foll 4th row.
64 (66: 68: 70: 72: 76) sts.
Cont straight until armhole measures 18 (19:
19: 20: 21: 22) cm, ending with a WS row.
Shape shoulders and back neck
Cast off 5 (5: 5: 5: 6: 6) sts at beg of next
2 rows.
54 (56: 58: 60: 60: 64) sts.
Next row (RS): Cast off 5 (5: 5: 5: 6: 6) sts,
patt until there are 9 (9: 10: 10: 9: 11) sts
on right needle and turn, leaving rem sts on
a holder.
Work each side of neck separately.
Cast off 4 sts at beg of next row.
Cast off rem 5 (5: 6: 6: 5: 7) sts.
With RS facing, rejoin yarn to rem sts, cast off
centre 26 (28: 28: 30: 30: 30) sts, patt to end.
Complete to match first side, reversing
shapings.

Pattern note: Row-end edges of fronts forms
actual front opening edges. To ensure edges
remains neat and tidy, make sure new balls of
yarn are joined in at side seam edges **only**.

LEFT FRONT

Cast on 40 (42: 45: 47: 50: 54) sts using
3¼mm (US 3) needles.
Work in g st as folls:
Work 4 rows, ending with a WS row.
Row 5 (RS): K7, K2tog tbl, K to last 7 sts,
yfwd, K7.
Work 3 rows.
Rep last 4 rows 8 times more, then row 5
again. 40 (42: 45: 47: 50: 54) sts.
Work 7 rows, ending with a WS row.
Change to 4mm (US 6) needles.
Beg and ending rows as indicated and
repeating the 20 row patt rep throughout,
cont in patt from chart for left front as folls:
Inc 1 st at beg of 7th and 2 foll 6th rows,
then on 4 foll 8th rows, taking inc sts into patt.
47 (49: 52: 54: 57: 61) sts.
Cont straight until left front matches back to
start of armhole shaping, ending with a WS row.
Shape armhole
Keeping patt correct, cast off 4 (4: 5: 5: 6: 6) sts
at beg of next row. 43 (45: 47: 49: 51: 55) sts.
Work 1 row.
Dec 1 st at armhole edge of next 3 (3: 5: 5: 7:
7) rows, then on foll 1 (2: 1: 2: 1: 3) alt rows,
then on foll 4th row.
38 (39: 40: 41: 42: 44) sts.
Cont straight until 34 (34: 34: 36: 36: 36) rows
less have been worked than on back to beg of
shoulder shaping, ending with a WS row.
Shape front neck
Next row (RS): Patt 28 (28: 29: 30: 31: 33)
sts and turn, leaving rem 10 (11: 11: 11: 11:
11) sts on a holder.
Keeping patt correct, dec 1 st at neck edge
of next 8 rows, then on foll 2 (2: 2: 3: 3: 3) alt
rows, then on foll 4th row, then on foll 6th row,
then on foll 8th row. 15 (15: 16: 16: 17: 19) sts.
Work 3 rows, ending with a WS row.
Shape shoulder
Cast off 5 (5: 5: 5: 6: 6) sts at beg of next
and foll alt row.
Work 1 row.
Cast off rem 5 (5: 6: 6: 5: 7) sts.
Mark positions for 5 buttons along left front
opening edge - first button to come level
with chart row 1, 5th button to come 3 rows
above neck shaping, and rem 3 buttons evenly
spaced between.

Back

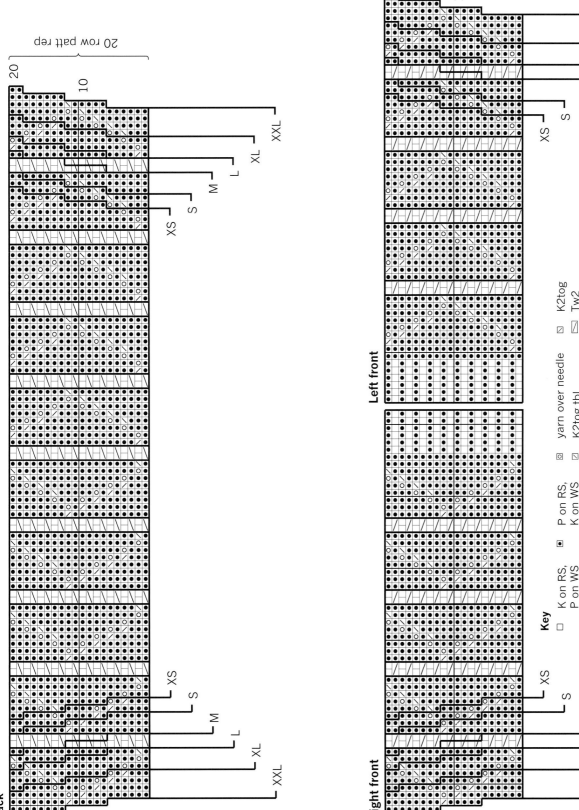

20 row patt rep

20

10

XXL
XL
L
M
S
XS

XS
S
M
L
XL
XXL

Left front

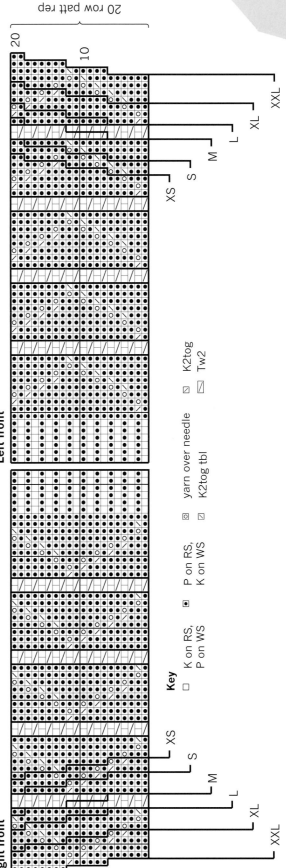

20 row patt rep

20

10

XS
S
M
L
XL
XXL

Right front

Key

☐ K on RS,
P on WS

▣ P on RS,
K on WS

◙ yarn over needle

▨ K2tog tbl

◪ K2tog

◺ Tw2

XS
S
M
L
XL
XXL

RIGHT FRONT

Cast on 40 (42: 45: 47: 50: 54) sts using 3¼mm (US 3) needles.
Work in g st as folls:
Work 4 rows, ending with a WS row.
Row 5 (RS): K7, yfwd, K to last 9 sts, K2tog, K7.
Work 3 rows.
Rep last 4 rows 8 times more, then row 5 again.
40 (42: 45: 47: 50: 54) sts.
Work 7 rows, ending with a WS row.
Change to 4mm (US 6) needles.
Beg and ending rows as indicated and repeating the 20 row patt rep throughout, cont in patt from chart for right front as folls:
Next row (buttonhole row) (RS): K2, K2tog tbl, yfwd (to make a buttonhole), patt to end.
Working a further 3 buttonholes in this way to correspond with positions marked for buttons on left front and noting that no further reference will be made to buttonholes, cont as folls:
Inc 1 st at end of 6th and 2 foll 6th rows, then on 4 foll 8th rows, taking inc sts into patt.
47 (49: 52: 54: 57: 61) sts.
Complete to match left front, reversing shapings and working first row of neck shaping as folls:

Shape front neck
Next row (RS): Patt 10 (11: 11: 11: 11: 11) sts and slip these sts onto a holder, patt to end.
28 (28: 29: 30: 31: 33) sts.

SLEEVES (both alike)

Cast on 38 (40: 42: 44: 46: 48) sts using 3¼mm (US 3) needles.
Work in g st for 10 rows, ending with a WS row.
Change to 4mm (US 6) needles.
Beg and ending rows as indicated and repeating the 20 row patt rep throughout, cont in patt from chart for sleeve as folls:
Inc 1 st at each end of 3rd and 4 (3: 1: 0: 4: 3) foll 10th rows, then on every foll 12th row until there are 60 (62: 64: 66: 70: 72) sts, taking inc sts into patt.
Cont straight until sleeve measures 48 (49: 50: 51: 52: 53) cm, ending with a WS row.

Shape top
Keeping patt correct, cast off 4 (4: 5: 5: 6: 6) sts at beg of next 2 rows.
52 (54: 54: 56: 58: 60) sts.
Dec 1 st at each end of next 3 rows, then on foll alt row, then on 5 foll 4th rows.
34 (36: 36: 38: 40: 42) sts.
Work 3 rows, ending with a WS row.
Dec 1 st at each end of next and every foll alt row to 30 sts, then on foll 5 rows, ending with a WS row.
Cast off rem 20 sts.

MAKING UP

Press all pieces with a warm iron over a damp cloth.
Join both shoulder seams using back stitch or mattress stitch if preferred.

Neckband
With RS facing and using 3¼mm (US 3) needles, slip 10 (11: 11: 11: 11: 11) sts on right front holder onto right needle, rejoin yarn and pick up and knit 32 (32: 32: 34: 34: 34) sts up right side of neck, 34 (36: 36: 38: 38: 38) sts from back, and 32 (32: 32: 34: 34: 34) sts down left side of neck, then patt 10 (11: 11: 11: 11: 11) sts on left front holder.
118 (122: 122: 128: 128: 128) sts.
Row 1 (WS): Knit.
Row 2: K2, K2tog tbl, yfwd (to make 5th buttonhole), patt to end.
Work in g st for a further 4 rows, ending with a **RS** row.
Cast off knitwise (on **WS**).
Join side seams. Join sleeve seams.
Insert sleeves into armholes.
Sew on buttons.

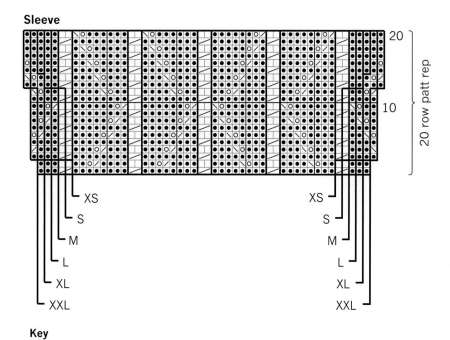

Sleeve

20
10
20 row patt rep

XS
S
M
L
XL
XXL

XS
S
M
L
XL
XXL

51 (52: 53: 54: 55: 56) cm
20 (21½: 21: 21¼: 21¾: 22) in

41 (43: 46: 48: 51: 55) cm
16 (17: 18: 19: 20: 21½) in

48 (49: 50: 51: 52: 53) cm
19 (19¼: 19¾: 20: 20½: 21) in

Key
□ K on RS, P on WS	⊡ P on RS, K on WS	▣ yarn over needle
	☑ K2tog tbl	◿ K2tog
		◺ Tw2

POOL
Textured boxy jacket

Recommendation
Suitable for the knitter with a little experience
Please see page 44 & 45 for photographs.

	XS	S	M	L	XL	XXL	
To fit	**81**	**86**	**91**	**97**	**102**	**109**	cm
bust	32	34	36	38	40	43	in

Rowan Denim
10 11 11 12 12 13 x 50gm
Photographed in Nashville

Needles
1 pair 3¾mm (no 9) (US 5) needles

Buttons – 6

Tension
Before washing: 23 sts and 32 rows to
10 cm measured over pattern using
3¾mm (US 5) needles.

Tension note: Denim will shrink in length
when washed for the first time. Allowances
have been made in the pattern for shrinkage
(see size diagram for after washing
measurements).

BACK
Cast on 101 (107: 113: 119: 125: 133) sts
using 3¾mm (US 5) needles.
Row 1 (WS): P0 (1: 0: 1: 0: 0), *K1, P1, rep
from * to last 1 (0: 1: 0: 1: 1) st, K1 (0: 1: 0:
1: 1).
Row 2: As row 1.
Rows 3 and 4: K0 (1: 0: 1: 0: 0), *P1, K1,
rep from * to last 1 (0: 1: 0: 1: 1) st, P1 (0: 1:
0: 1: 1).
These 4 rows form double moss st.
Work in double moss st for a further 17 rows,
ending with a WS row.
Beg and ending rows as indicated, working
chart rows 1 to 6 **once only** and then
repeating chart rows 7 to 22 **throughout**, cont
in patt from chart as folls:
Work straight until back measures 26.5 (26.5:
27.5: 27.5: 27.5: 27.5) cm, ending with
a WS row.
Shape armholes
Keeping patt correct, cast off 5 (5: 6: 6: 7: 7)
sts at beg of next 2 rows.
91 (97: 101: 107: 111: 119) sts.
Dec 1 st at each end of next 3 (3: 5: 5: 7: 7)
rows, then on foll 2 (4: 3: 5: 4: 6) alt rows,
then on foll 4th row.
79 (81: 83: 85: 87: 91) sts.
Cont straight until armhole measures 20.5
(21.5: 21.5: 22.5: 23.5: 25) cm, ending with
a WS row.
Shape shoulders and back neck
Cast off 7 (7: 8: 8: 8: 9) sts at beg of next
2 rows. 65 (67: 67: 69: 71: 73) sts.
Next row (RS): Cast off 7 (7: 8: 8: 8: 9) sts,
patt until there are 12 (12: 11: 11: 12: 12) sts
on right needle and turn, leaving rem sts on
a holder.
Work each side of neck separately.
Cast off 4 sts at beg of next row.
Cast off rem 8 (8: 7: 7: 8: 8) sts.
With RS facing, rejoin yarn to rem sts, cast off
centre 27 (29: 29: 31: 31: 31) sts, patt to end.
Complete to match first side, reversing
shapings.

Pattern note: Row-end edges of fronts forms
actual front opening edges. To ensure edges
remains neat and tidy, make sure new balls of
yarn are joined in at side seam edges **only**.

LEFT FRONT
Cast on 56 (59: 62: 65: 68: 72) sts using
3¾mm (US 5) needles.
Row 1 (WS): (P1, K1) 5 times, P1, K2, *K1, P1,
rep from * to last 1 (0: 1: 0: 1: 1) st, K1 (0: 1:
0: 1: 1).
Row 2: P0 (1: 0: 1: 0: 0), *K1, P1, rep from *
to end.
Row 3: (P1, K1) 5 times, P1, K2, *P1, K1, rep
from * to last 1 (0: 1: 0: 1: 1) st, P1 (0: 1: 0:
1: 1).
Row 4: K0 (1: 0: 1: 0: 0), *P1, K1, rep from *
to last 14 sts, P2, (K1, P1) 6 times.
These 4 rows set the sts - front opening edge
13 st border and rem sts in double moss st.
Cont as set for a further 17 rows, ending with
a WS row.
Beg and ending rows as indicated, working
chart rows 1 to 6 **once only** and then
repeating chart rows 7 to 22 **throughout**, cont
in patt from chart as folls:
Row 1 (RS): Work first 43 (46: 49: 52: 55: 59)
sts as row 1 of chart, patt 13 sts.
Row 2: Patt 13 sts, work rem 43 (46: 49: 52:
55: 59) sts as row 2 of chart.
These 2 rows set the sts - front opening edge
13 sts still in border patt and rem sts now in
patt from chart.
Cont as now set straight until left front matches
back to start of armhole shaping, ending with
a WS row.
Shape armhole
Keeping patt correct, cast off 5 (5: 6: 6: 7: 7) sts
at beg of next row. 51 (54: 56: 59: 61: 65) sts.
Work 1 row.
Dec 1 st at armhole edge of next 3 (3: 5: 5: 7:
7) rows, then on foll 2 (4: 3: 5: 4: 6) alt rows,
then on foll 4th row. 45 (46: 47: 48: 49: 51) sts.
Cont straight until 18 (18: 18: 20: 20: 20) rows
less have been worked than on back to start
of shoulder shaping, ending with a WS row.
Shape front neck
Next row (RS): Patt 32 (32: 33: 34: 35: 37)
sts and turn, leaving rem 13 (14: 14: 14: 14:
14) sts on a holder.
Keeping patt correct, dec 1 st at neck edge of
next 6 rows, then on foll 3 (3: 3: 4: 4: 4) alt
rows, then on foll 4th row.
22 (22: 23: 23: 24: 26) sts.
Work 1 row, ending with a WS row.

Shape shoulder

Cast off 7 (7: 8: 8: 8: 9) sts at beg of next and foll alt row.

Work 1 row.

Cast off rem 8 (8: 7: 7: 8: 8) sts.

Mark positions for 6 buttons along left front opening edge - first button to come level with chart row 5, 6th button to come just above start of front neck shaping, and rem 4 buttons evenly spaced between.

RIGHT FRONT

Cast on 56 (59: 62: 65: 68: 72) sts using 3¾mm (US 5) needles.

Row 1 (WS): K1 (0: 1: 0: 1: 1), *P1, K1, rep from * to last 13 sts, K2, P1, (K1, P1) 5 times.

Row 2: *P1, K1, rep from * to last 0 (1: 0: 1: 0: 0) st, P0 (1: 0: 1: 0: 0).

Row 3: P1 (0: 1: 0: 1: 1), *K1, P1, rep from * to last 13 sts, K2, P1, (K1, P1) 5 times.

Row 4: (P1, K1) 6 times, P2, *K1, P1, rep from * to last 0 (1: 0: 1: 0: 0) st, K0 (1: 0: 1: 0: 0).

These 4 rows set the sts - front opening edge 13 st border and rem sts in double moss st.

Cont as set st for a further 17 rows, ending with a WS row.

Beg and ending rows as indicated, working chart rows 1 to 6 **once only** and then repeating chart rows 7 to 22 **throughout**, cont in patt from chart as folls:

Row 1 (RS): Patt 13 sts, work rem 43 (46: 49: 52: 55: 59) sts as row 1 of chart.

Row 2: Work first 43 (46: 49: 52: 55: 59) sts as row 2 of chart, patt 13 sts.

These 2 rows set the sts - front opening edge 13 sts still in border patt and rem sts now in patt from chart.

Keeping sts correct as now set, work 2 rows, ending with a WS row.

Row 5 (buttonhole row) (RS): Patt 5 sts, work 2 tog, yrn (to make a buttonhole), patt to end.

Making a further 4 buttonholes in this way to correspond with positions marked for buttons on left front and noting that no further reference will be made to buttonholes, cont as folls:

Complete to match left front, reversing shapings and working first row of neck shaping as folls:

Shape front neck

Next row (RS): Patt 13 (14: 14: 14: 14: 14) sts and slip these sts onto a holder, patt to end.

32 (32: 33: 34: 35: 37) sts.

SLEEVES (both alike)

Cast on 55 (57: 59: 61: 63: 65) sts using 3¾mm (US 5) needles.

Row 1 (WS): P1 (0: 1: 0: 1: 0), *K1, P1, rep from * to last 0 (1: 0: 1: 0: 1) st, K0 (1: 0: 1: 0: 1).

Row 2: As row 1.

Rows 3 and 4: K1 (0: 1: 0: 1: 0), *P1, K1, rep from * to last 0 (1: 0: 1: 0: 1) st, P0 (1: 0: 1: 0: 1).

These 4 rows form double moss st.

Work in double moss st for a further 17 rows, inc 1 st at each end of 12th of these rows and ending with a WS row.

57 (59: 61: 63: 65: 67) sts.

Beg and ending rows as indicated, working chart rows 1 to 6 **once only** and then repeating chart rows 7 to 22 **throughout**, cont in patt from chart as folls:

Inc 1 st at each end of 3rd (3rd: 3rd: 5th: 3rd: 3rd) and every foll 10th (10th: 12th: 12th: 10th: 12th) row to 65 (65: 75: 75: 71: 83) sts, then on every foll 12th (12th: -: 14th: 12th: -) row until there are 71 (73: -: 77: 81: -) sts, taking inc sts into patt.

Cont straight until sleeve measures 33 (34: 35: 36.5: 37.5: 38.5) cm, ending with a WS row.

Shape top

Keeping patt correct, cast off 5 (5: 6: 6: 7: 7) sts at beg of next 2 rows.

61 (63: 63: 65: 67: 69) sts.

Dec 1 st at each end of next 3 rows, then on foll alt row, then on foll 4th row, then on 3 foll 6th rows, then on 2 foll 4th rows.

41 (43: 43: 45: 47: 49) sts.

Work 1 row.

Dec 1 st at each end of next and every foll alt row until 35 sts rem, then on foll 5 rows, ending with a WS row.

Cast off rem 25 sts.

MAKING UP

Do NOT press.

Join both shoulder seams using back stitch or mattress stitch if preferred.

Neckband

With RS facing and using 3¾mm (US 5) needles, slip 13 (14: 14: 14: 14: 14) sts on right front holder onto right needle, rejoin yarn and pick up and knit 19 (19: 19: 21: 21: 21) sts up right side of neck, 35 (37: 37: 39: 39: 39) sts from back, and 19 (19: 19: 21: 21: 21) sts down left side of neck, then patt 13 (14: 14: 14: 14: 14) sts on left front holder.

99 (103: 103: 109: 109: 109) sts.

Row 1 (WS): Patt 13 sts, K1, *P1, K1, rep from * to last 13 sts, patt 13 sts.

Row 2: As row 1.

These 2 rows set the sts - front opening edge 13 sts in patt as set by fronts and rem sts in moss st.

Keeping sts correct as set, cont as folls:

Work 1 row.

Row 4 (RS): Patt 5 sts, work 2 tog, yrn (to make 6th buttonhole), patt to end.

Cont as set for a further 7 rows, ending with a WS row.

Cast off in patt.

Machine wash all pieces together before completing sewing up.

Join side seams. Join sleeve seams. Insert sleeves into armholes. Sew on buttons.

After washing measurements:

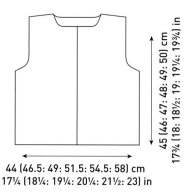

45 (46: 47: 48: 49: 50) cm
17¾ (18: 18½: 19: 19¼: 19¾) in

44 (46.5: 49: 51.5: 54.5: 58) cm
17¼ (18¼: 19¼: 20¼: 21½: 23) in

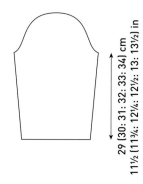

29 (30: 31: 32: 33: 34) cm
11½ (11¾: 12¼: 12½: 13: 13½) in

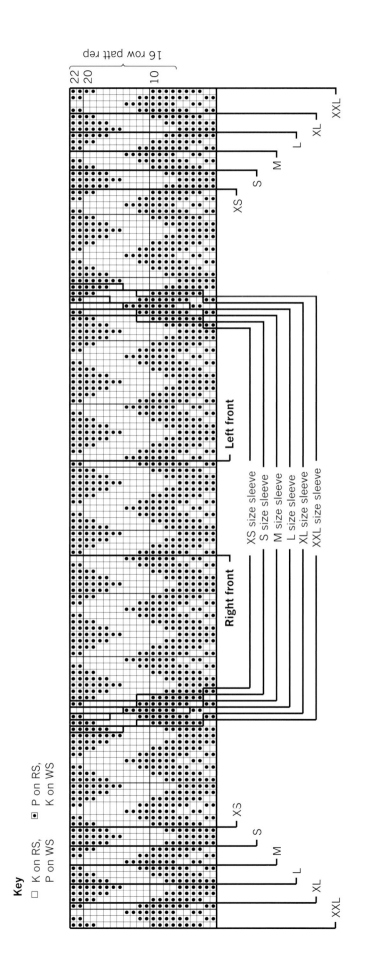

Key

□ K on RS,   ⊡ P on RS,
  P on WS   K on WS

16 row patt rep

22
20
10

XS
S
M
L
XL
XXL

Left front

Right front

XS size sleeve
S size sleeve
M size sleeve
L size sleeve
XL size sleeve
XXL size sleeve

XS
S
M
L
XL
XXL

SAND

Wide sweater worked in a textured pattern

Recommendation

Suitable for the knitter with a little experience
Please see pages 38 & 39 for photographs.

	XS	S	M	L	XL	XXL	
To fit	**81**	**86**	**91**	**97**	**102**	**109**	cm
bust	32	34	36	38	40	43	in

Rowan Handknit Cotton

| 10 | 11 | 11 | 12 | 12 | 13 | x 50gm |

Photographed in Ochre

Needles

1 pair 3¾mm (no 9) (US 5) needles
1 pair 4mm (no 8) (US 6) needles

Tension

20 sts and 28 rows to 10 cm measured over
pattern using 4mm (US 6) needles.

BACK

Cast on 103 (107: 113: 117: 123: 131) sts
using 3¾mm (US 5) needles.
Row 1 (WS): P1 (1: 0: 0: 1: 1), *K1, P1, rep
from * to last 0 (0: 1: 1: 0: 0) st, K0 (0: 1: 1:
0: 0).
Row 2: As row 1.
Row 3: K1 (1: 0: 0: 1: 1), *P1, K1, rep from
* to last 0 (0: 1: 1: 0: 0) st, P0 (0: 1: 1: 0: 0).
Row 4: As row 3.
These 4 rows form double moss st.
Work in double moss st for a further 15 (15:
15: 19: 19: 19) rows, ending with a WS row.
Change to 4mm (US 6) needles.
Beg and ending rows as indicated, working
chart rows 1 to 6 **once only** and then
repeating chart rows 7 to 22 **throughout**,
cont in patt from chart for back as folls:
Cont straight until back measures 25 (25: 26:
26: 27: 27) cm, ending with a WS row.
Shape armholes
Keeping patt correct, cast off 5 sts at beg of
next 2 rows.
93 (97: 103: 107: 113: 121) sts.
Cont straight until chart rows 7 to 22 have
been worked 6 times in total, ending with
a WS row.
Now working chart rows 23 to 30 **once only**
and then repeating chart rows 31 to 34 as
required, cont as folls:
Cont straight until armhole measures 22 (23:
23: 24: 24: 25) cm, ending with a **RS** row.**
Shape shoulders and back neck
Next row (WS): Patt 17 (18: 21: 22: 25:
29) sts and slip these sts onto a holder
for left shoulder, cast off next 59 (61: 61:
63: 63: 63) sts (for back neck), patt to
end and slip this last set of 17 (18: 21:
22: 25: 29) sts onto another holder for
right shoulder.
Break yarn.

FRONT

Work as given for back to **.
Work 1 row, ending with a WS row.
Shape shoulders and front neck
Now holding back and front together with WS
facing (so shoulder cast-off edges form a ridge
on RS of garment), cast off sts of shoulders
together and front neck as folls:

Next row (RS): Taking one st from front with
corresponding st of left back shoulder, cast
off first 17 (18: 21: 22: 25: 29) sts (for left
shoulder seam), cast off next 59 (61: 61: 63:
63: 63) sts of front (for front neck), then cast
off rem 17 (18: 21: 22: 25: 29) sts of front
with corresponding sts of right back shoulder
(for right shoulder seam).

SLEEVES (both alike)

Cast on 61 (63: 65: 67: 69: 71) sts using
3¾mm (US 5) needles.
Row 1 (WS): P1 (0: 1: 0: 1: 0), *K1, P1, rep
from * to last 0 (1: 0: 1: 0: 1) st, K0 (1: 0: 1:
0: 1).
Row 2: As row 1.
Row 3: K1 (0: 1: 0: 1: 0), *P1, K1, rep from
* to last 0 (1: 0: 1: 0: 1) st, P0 (1: 0: 1: 0: 1).
Row 4: As row 3.
These 4 rows form double moss st.
Cont in double moss st, inc 1 st at each
end of 6th and 0 (0: 0: 1: 1: 1) foll 6th row,
taking inc sts into patt.
63 (65: 67: 71: 73: 75) sts.
Work 3 (3: 3: 1: 1: 1) rows, ending with
a WS row.
Change to 4mm (US 6) needles.
Beg and ending rows as indicated,
working chart rows 1 to 6 **once only**
and then repeating chart rows 7 to
22 **throughout**, cont in patt from chart
for sleeve as folls:
Inc 1 st at each end of 3rd (3rd: 3rd:
5th: 5th: 5th) and 9 (7: 9: 8: 10: 8) foll
6th rows, then on 3 (6: 3: 4: 1: 4) foll
4th rows, taking inc sts into patt.
89 (93: 93: 97: 97: 101) sts.
Work 6 rows, ending with a **RS** row.
Shape top
Place markers at both ends of last row to
denote top of sleeve seam.
Work 7 rows, ending after chart row 18 and
with a WS row.
Working chart rows 19 to 22 as set and then
completing sleeve in st st, beg with a K row,
cont as folls:
Cast off 5 (6: 6: 6: 6: 7) sts at beg of next
4 rows, then 6 (6: 6: 7: 7: 7) sts at beg of
foll 4 rows.
Cast off rem 45 sts.

MAKING UP

Press all pieces with a warm iron over a damp cloth.

Matching sleeve markers to top of side seams and shaped sleeve cast-off edge to row-end edges of armhole, sew sleeves to back and front. Join side and sleeve seams.

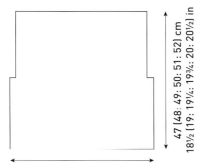

51.5 (53.5: 56.5: 58.5: 61.5: 65.5) cm
20¼ (21: 22: 23: 24¼: 25½) in

47 (48: 49: 50: 51: 52) cm
18½ (19: 19¼: 19¾: 20: 20½) in

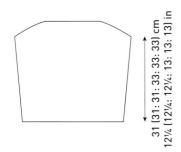

31 (31: 31: 33: 33: 33) cm
12¼ (12¼: 12¼: 13: 13: 13) in

Key

☐ K on RS, P on WS

⊡ P on RS, K on WS

Body and sleeve chart

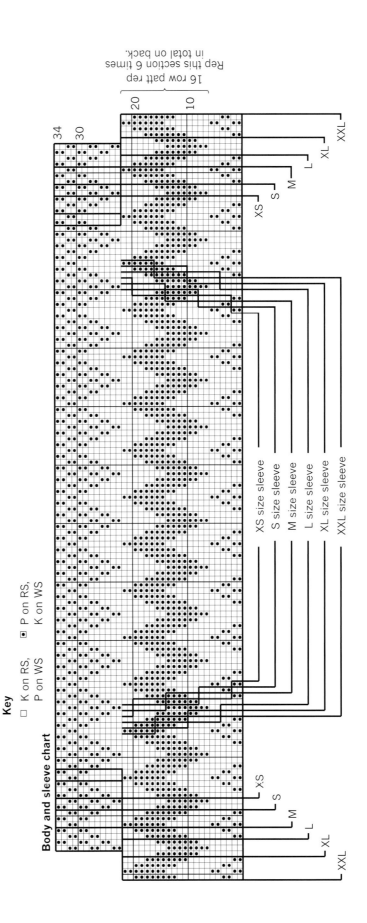

Rep this section 6 times in total on back.

16 row patt rep

XS size sleeve
S size sleeve
M size sleeve
L size sleeve
XL size sleeve
XXL size sleeve

XS
S
M
L
XL
XXL

SCORCHED

Close-fitting textured sweater dress

Recommendation

Suitable for the knitter with a little experience
Please see pages 42 & 43 for photographs.

	XS	S	M	L	XL	XXL	
To fit	**81**	**86**	**91**	**97**	**102**	**109**	cm
bust	32	34	36	38	40	43	in

Rowan All Seasons Cotton

      12   12   13   14   15   16 x 50gm
Photographed in Storm

Needles

1 pair 4mm (no 8) (US 6) needles
1 pair 4½mm (no 7) (US 7) needles

Tension

19 sts and 27 rows to 10 cm measured over
pattern using 4½mm (US 7) needles.

BACK and FRONT (both alike)

Cast on 85 (89: 93: 99: 103: 111) sts using
4mm (US 6) needles.
Row 1 (WS): P1 (1: 1: 0: 0: 0), *K1, P1, rep
from * to last 0 (0: 0: 1: 1: 1) st, K0 (0: 0: 1:
1: 1).
Row 2: As row 1.
Row 3: K1 (1: 1: 0: 0: 0), *P1, K1, rep from
* to last 0 (0: 0: 1: 1: 1) st, P0 (0: 0: 1: 1: 1).
Row 4: As row 3.
These 4 rows form double moss st.
Work in double moss st for a further
17 (17: 21: 21: 21: 21) rows, ending
with a WS row.
Change to 4½mm (US 7) needles.
Beg and ending rows as indicated, working
chart rows 1 to 6 **once only** and then
repeating chart rows 7 to 22 **throughout**,
cont in patt from chart for body as folls:
Work 22 (22: 20: 20: 20: 20) rows, ending
with a WS row.
Keeping patt correct, dec 1 st at each end
of next and foll 10th row, then on foll 8th
row, then on 5 foll 6th rows.
69 (73: 77: 83: 87: 95) sts.
Work 17 rows, ending with a WS row.
Inc 1 st at each end of next and 6 foll 6th
rows, taking inc sts into patt.
83 (87: 91: 97: 101: 109) sts.
Cont straight until work measures 56 (56: 57:
57: 57: 57) cm, ending with a WS row.

Shape armholes

Keeping patt correct, cast off 4 (4: 5: 5: 6: 6)
sts at beg of next 2 rows.
75 (79: 81: 87: 89: 97) sts.
Dec 1 st at each end of next 3 (5: 5: 7: 7: 9)
rows, then on foll 3 (2: 2: 2: 2: 3) alt rows,
then on foll 4th row.
61 (63: 65: 67: 69: 71) sts.
Cont straight until chart rows 7 to 22 have
been worked 10 times in total, ending with
a WS row.
Now working chart rows 23 to 28 **once only**
and then repeating chart rows 29 to 32 as
required, cont as folls:
Cont straight until armhole measures 18 (19:
19: 20: 21: 22) cm, ending with a WS row.
Cast off all sts in patt, placing markers
4 (4: 5: 5: 6: 7) sts in from ends of row
to denote neck opening.

SLEEVES (both alike)

Cast on 43 (45: 47: 49: 51: 53) sts using
4mm (US 6) needles.
Row 1 (WS): P1 (0: 1: 0: 1: 0), *K1, P1, rep
from * to last 0 (1: 0: 1: 0: 1) st, K0 (1: 0: 1:
0: 1).
Row 2: As row 1.
Row 3: K1 (0: 1: 0: 1: 0), *P1, K1, rep from
* to last 0 (1: 0: 1: 0: 1) st, P0 (1: 0: 1: 0: 1).
Row 4: As row 3.
These 4 rows form double moss st.
Cont in double moss st for a further 7 rows,
ending with a WS row.
Change to 4½mm (US 7) needles.
Beg and ending rows as indicated, working
chart rows 1 to 6 **once only** and then
repeating chart rows 7 to 22 **throughout**,
cont in patt from chart for sleeve as folls:
Inc 1 st at each end of next and every foll
8th (8th: 8th: 10th: 8th: 8th) row to 53 (51:
51: 63: 59: 59) sts, then on every foll 10th
(10th: 10th: 12th: 10th: 10th) row until there
are 59 (61: 63: 65: 69: 71) sts, taking inc sts
into patt.
Cont straight until sleeve measures 32 (33: 34:
35: 36: 37) cm, ending with a WS row.

Shape top

Keeping patt correct, cast off 4 (4: 5: 5: 6: 6)
sts at beg of next 2 rows.
51 (53: 53: 55: 57: 59) sts.
Dec 1 st at each end of next 3 rows, then on
foll alt row, then on 5 foll 4th rows.
33 (35: 35: 37: 39: 41) sts.
Work 1 row.
Dec 1 st at each end of next and every foll alt
row to 29 sts, then on foll 5 rows, ending with
a WS row.
Cast off rem 19 sts.

MAKING UP

Press all pieces with a warm iron over
a damp cloth.
Join both shoulder seams using back stitch
or mattress stitch if preferred, leaving opening
for neck between markers.
Join side seams. Join sleeve seams.
Insert sleeves into armholes.

74 (75: 76: 77: 78: 79) cm
29 (29½: 20: 30¼: 30¾: 31) in

43.5 (46: 48: 51: 53: 57.5) cm
17 (18: 19: 20: 21: 22½) in

32 (33: 34: 35: 36: 37) cm
12½ (13: 13¼: 13¾: 14¼: 14½) in

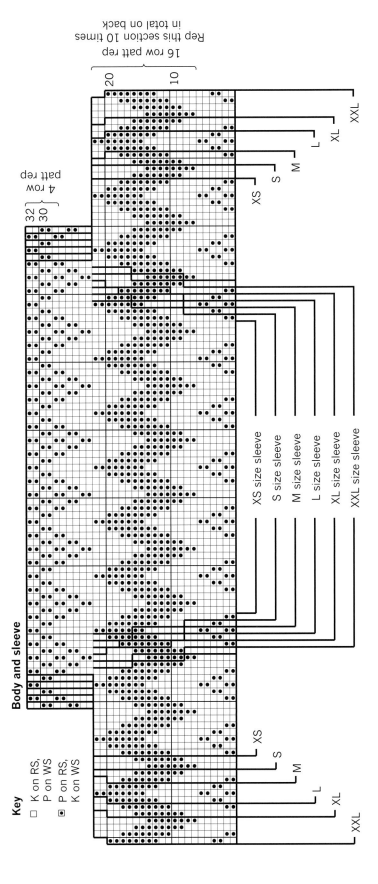

Body and sleeve

Rep this section 10 times
in total on back

16 row patt rep

20

10

XXL
XL
L
M
S
XS

4 row patt rep

32
30

XS size sleeve
S size sleeve
M size sleeve
L size sleeve
XL size sleeve
XXL size sleeve

XS
S
M
L
XL
XXL

Key

☐ K on RS,
P on WS
▣ P on RS,
K on WS

BRONZE
Classic sweater with textured stripe

Recommendation
Suitable for the knitter with a little experience
Please see pages 46 & 47 for photographs.

	XS	S	M	L	XL	XXL	
To fit	**81**	**86**	**91**	**97**	**102**	**109**	cm
bust	32	34	36	38	40	43	in

Rowan Pima Cotton DK

| 7 | 8 | 8 | 9 | 9 | 10 | x 50gm |

Photographed in Fig

Needles
1 pair 3mm (no 11) (US 2/3) needles
1 pair 3¾mm (no 9) (US 5) needles

Tension
21 sts and 24 rows to 10 cm measured over
pattern using 3¾mm (US 5) needles.

BACK
Cast on 90 (94: 102: 106: 110: 118) sts using
3mm (US 2/3) needles.
Row 1 (RS): K2, *P2, K2, rep from * to end.
Row 2: P2, *K2, P2, rep from * to end.
These 2 rows form rib.
Cont in rib until back measures 5 cm, inc
0 (1: 0: 0: 1: 1) st at each end of last row
and ending with a WS row.
90 (96: 102: 106: 112: 120) sts.
Change to 3¾mm (US 5) needles.
Now work in patt as folls:
Row 1 (RS): Purl.
Row 2: Knit.
Rows 3 and 4: As rows 1 and 2.
Row 5: Purl, winding yarn twice round needle
for each st.
Row 6: Knit, dropping extra loops.
These 6 rows form patt.
Keeping patt correct, cont as folls:
Next row (dec) (RS): P8, P2tog tbl, P to last
10 sts, P2tog, P8.
Work 5 rows.
Rep last 6 rows 4 times more, then first of
these rows (the dec row) again.
78 (84: 90: 94: 100: 108) sts.
Work 13 rows, ending with a WS row.
Next row (inc) (RS): P3, M1 purlwise, P to last
3 sts, M1 purlwise, P3.
Work 5 rows.
Rep last 6 rows 4 times more, then first of
these rows (the inc row) again.
90 (96: 102: 106: 112: 120) sts.
Cont straight until back measures 43 (43: 44:
44: 44: 44) cm, ending with a WS row.
Shape armholes
Keeping patt correct, cast off 4 (4: 5: 5: 6: 6)
sts at beg of next 2 rows.
82 (88: 92: 96: 100: 108) sts.
Dec 1 st at each end of next 3 (5: 5: 7: 7: 9)
rows, then on foll 3 (3: 4: 3: 4: 4) alt rows,
then on foll 4th row. 68 (70: 72: 74: 76: 80) sts.
Cont straight until armhole measures 18 (19:
19: 20: 21: 22) cm, ending with a WS row.
Shape shoulders and back neck
Cast off 4 (4: 4: 4: 4: 5) sts at beg of next
2 rows. 60 (62: 64: 66: 68: 70) sts.
Next row (RS): Cast off 4 (4: 4: 4: 4: 5) sts,
patt until there are 7 (7: 8: 8: 9: 9) sts on right
needle and turn, leaving rem sts on a holder.

Work each side of neck separately.
Cast off 4 sts at beg of next row.
Cast off rem 3 (3: 4: 4: 5: 5) sts.
With RS facing, rejoin yarn to rem sts, cast off
centre 38 (40: 40: 42: 42: 42) sts, patt to end.
Complete to match first side, reversing
shapings.

FRONT
Work as given for back until 18 (18: 18: 20:
20: 20) rows less have been worked than on
back to start of shoulder shaping, ending with
a WS row.
Shape front neck
Next row (RS): Patt 21 (21: 22: 23: 24: 26)
sts and turn, leaving rem sts on a holder.
Work each side of neck separately.
Keeping patt correct, dec 1 st at neck edge
of next 6 rows, then on foll 3 (3: 3: 4: 4: 4)
alt rows, then on foll 4th row.
11 (11: 12: 12: 13: 15) sts.
Work 1 row, ending with a WS row.
Shape shoulder
Cast off 4 (4: 4: 4: 4: 5) sts at beg of next
and foll alt row.
Work 1 row, ending with a WS row.
Cast off rem 3 (3: 4: 4: 5: 5) sts.
With RS facing, rejoin yarn to rem sts, cast off
centre 26 (28: 28: 28: 28: 28) sts, patt to end.
Complete to match first side, reversing
shapings.

SLEEVES (both alike)
Cast on 37 (39: 41: 43: 45: 47) sts using
3mm (US 2/3) needles.
Starting with a P row, now work in reverse st st
for 8 rows, ending with a WS row.
Starting with patt row 5, now work in patt
as given for back as folls:
Work 2 rows, ending with a WS row.
Change to 3¾mm (US 5) needles.
Working all increases in same way as side
seam increases, cont in patt, shaping sides by
inc 1 st at each end of 5th and every foll 8th
(8th: 10th: 10th: 8th: 8th) row to 43 (43: 63:
63: 51: 51) sts, then on every foll 10th (10th:
12th: 12th: 10th: 10th) row until there are 61
(63: 65: 67: 71: 73) sts, taking inc sts into patt.
Cont straight until sleeve measures 51 (52: 53:
54: 55: 56) cm, ending with a WS row.

Shape top

Keeping patt correct, cast off 4 (4: 5: 5: 6: 6) sts at beg of next 2 rows. 53 (55: 55: 57: 59: 61) sts.

Dec 1 st at each end of next 3 rows, then on foll alt row, then on 4 foll 4th rows. 37 (39: 39: 41: 43: 45) sts.

Work 1 row.

Dec 1 st at each end of next and every foll alt row until 29 sts rem, then on foll 3 rows, ending with a WS row.

Cast off rem 23 sts.

MAKING UP

Press all pieces with a warm iron over a damp cloth.

Join right shoulder seam using back stitch or mattress stitch if preferred.

Neckband

With RS facing and using 3mm (US 2/3) needles, pick up and knit 23 (23: 23: 26: 26: 26) down left side of neck, 26 (28: 28: 28: 28: 28) sts from front, 23 (23: 23: 26: 26: 26) sts up right side of neck, then 46 (48: 48: 50: 50: 50) from back.

118 (122: 122: 130: 130: 130) sts.

Starting with row 2, work in rib as given for back for 7 rows, ending with a WS row.

Cast off in rib.

Join left shoulder and neckband seam. Join side seams. Join sleeve seams. Insert sleeves into armholes.

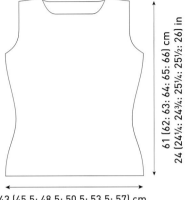

61 (62: 63: 64: 65: 66) cm
24 (24¼: 24¾: 25¼: 25½: 26) in

43 (45.5: 48.5: 50.5: 53.5: 57) cm
17 (18: 19: 20: 21: 22½) in

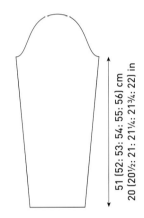

51 (52: 53: 54: 55: 56) cm
20 (20½: 21: 21¼: 21¾: 22) in

SHEEN

Classic sweater with beading & keyhole back

Recommendation

Suitable for the knitter with a little experience
Please see pages 48, 49 & 51 for photographs.

	XS	S	M	L	XL	XXL	
To fit	**81**	**86**	**91**	**97**	**102**	**109**	cm
bust	32	34	36	38	40	43	in

Rowan Siena 4 ply

6 7 7 8 8 9 x 50gm

Photographed in Starry

Needles

1 pair 2mm (no 14) (US 0) needles
1 pair 2¾mm (no 12) (US 2) needles
2.50mm (no 12) (US C2) crochet hook

Buttons - 2

Beads - approx 2160 (2320: 2550: 2720: 2940: 3190) size 8 beads

Tension

28 sts and 38 rows to 10 cm measured over stocking stitch, 30 sts and 41 rows to 10 cm measured over beaded stocking stitch, both using 2¾mm (US 2) needles.

SPECIAL ABBREVIATIONS

bead 1 = place a bead by taking yarn to RS of work and slipping bead up next to st just worked, slip next st purlwise from left needle to right needle and take yarn back to WS of work, leaving bead sitting in front of slipped st on RS. See page 98 for further details.

BACK

Cast on 114 (122: 130: 134: 142: 154) sts using 2mm (US 0) needles.
Row 1 (RS): K2, *P2, K2, rep from * to end.
Row 2: P2, *K2, P2, rep from * to end.
These 2 rows form rib.
Cont in rib until back measures 6 cm, inc (dec: dec: inc: inc: dec) 1 st at centre of last row and ending with a WS row.
115 (121: 129: 135: 143: 153) sts.
Change to 2¾mm (US 2) needles.
Beg with a K row, work in st st until back measures 33 (33: 34: 34: 34: 34) cm, ending with a WS row.

Shape armholes

Cast off 6 (6: 7: 7: 8: 8) sts at beg of next 2 rows. 103 (109: 115: 121: 127: 137) sts.
Dec 1 st at each end of next 3 (3: 5: 5: 7: 7) rows, then on foll 2 (4: 4: 5: 5: 8) alt rows, then on foll 4th row. 91 (93: 95: 99: 101: 105) sts.
Cont straight until armhole measures 7.5 (8.5: 8.5: 9.5: 10.5: 11.5) cm, ending with a WS row.

Divide for back opening

Next row (RS): K42 (43: 44: 46: 47: 49) and turn, leaving rem sts on a holder.
Work each side of back separately.
Next row (WS): P2, P2tog tbl, P to end.
Next row: K to last 4 sts, K2tog tbl, K2.
Work 1 row.
Next row: K to last 4 sts, K2tog tbl, K2.
39 (40: 41: 43: 44: 46) sts.
Work 9 rows, ending with a WS row.
Next row (RS): K to last 2 sts, M1, K2.
Working all increases as set by last row, inc 1 st at back opening edge of 4th and 3 foll 4th rows. 44 (45: 46: 48: 49: 51) sts.
Work 5 rows, ending with a WS row.

Shape shoulder and back neck

Cast off 7 (7: 7: 8: 8: 9) sts at beg and inc 1 st at end of next row.
Cast off 20 (21: 21: 22: 22: 22) sts at beg of next row, 7 (7: 7: 8: 8: 9) sts at beg of foll row, then 4 sts at beg of next row.
Cast off rem 7 (7: 8: 7: 8: 8) sts.
With RS facing, rejoin yarn to rem sts, cast off centre 7 sts, K to end.
42 (43: 44: 46: 47: 49) sts.
Next row (WS): P to last 4 sts, P2tog, P2.
Next row: K2, K2tog, K to end.
Work 1 row.

Next row: K2, K2tog, K to end.
39 (40: 41: 43: 44: 46) sts.
Work 9 rows, ending with a WS row.
Next row (RS): K2, M1, K to end.
Complete to match first side, reversing shapings.

FRONT

Cast on 114 (122: 130: 134: 142: 154) sts using 2mm (US 0) needles.
Work in rib as given for back for 6 cm, ending with a RS row.
Next row (WS): Rib 5 (10: 5: 7: 6: 9), M1, *rib 13 (17: 15: 12: 13: 17), M1, rep from * to last 5 (10: 5: 7: 6: 9) sts, rib 5 (10: 5: 7: 6: 9).
123 (129: 139: 145: 153: 163) sts.
Change to 2¾mm (US 2) needles.
Beg with a K row, work in st st for 2 rows, ending with a WS row.
Beg and ending rows as indicated and repeating the 44 row patt rep throughout, cont in patt from chart for front as folls:
Cont straight until front matches back to start of armhole shaping, ending with a WS row.

Shape armholes

Keeping patt correct, cast off 7 (7: 8: 8: 9: 9) sts at beg of next 2 rows.
109 (115: 123: 129: 135: 145) sts.
Dec 1 st at each end of next 3 (3: 5: 5: 7: 7) rows, then on foll 2 (4: 4: 5: 5: 8) alt rows, then on foll 4th row.
97 (99: 103: 107: 109: 113) sts.
Cont straight until armhole measures 11.5 (12.5: 12.5: 12.5: 13.5: 14.5) cm, ending with a WS row.

Shape front neck

Next row (RS): Patt 34 (34: 36: 38: 39: 41) sts and turn, leaving rem sts on a holder.
Keeping patt correct, dec 1 st at neck edge of next 6 rows, then on foll 5 alt rows, then on 1 (1: 1: 2: 2: 2) foll 4th rows.
22 (22: 24: 25: 26: 28) sts.
Work 1 row, ending with RS facing for next row.

Shape shoulder

Cast off 7 (7: 8: 8: 9: 9) sts at beg of next and foll alt row.
Work 1 row.
Cast off rem 8 (8: 8: 9: 8: 10) sts.
With RS facing, rejoin yarn to rem sts, cast off centre 29 (31: 31: 31: 31: 31) sts, patt to end.
Complete to match first side, reversing shapings.

SLEEVES (both alike)

Cast on 78 (82: 82: 86: 90: 90) sts using
2mm (US 0) needles.
Work in rib as given for back for 8 rows,
ending with a WS row.
Inc 1 st at each end of next row.
80 (84: 84: 88: 92: 92) sts.
Work a further 5 rows in rib, inc (dec: inc: dec:
dec: inc) 1 st at centre of last row and ending
with a WS row. 81 (83: 85: 87: 91: 93) sts.
Change to 2¾mm (US 2) needles.
Next row (RS): Inc in first st, K to last st, inc
in last st. 83 (85: 87: 89: 93: 95) sts.
Next row: Purl.
Next row: K5 (2: 3: 4: 2: 3), bead 1, *K7, bead
1, rep from * to last 5 (2: 3: 4: 2: 3) sts, K5 (2:
3: 4: 2: 3).
Beg with a P row, cont in st st as folls:
Work 3 rows, ending with a WS row.

Shape top

Cast off 6 (6: 7: 7: 8: 8) sts at beg of next
2 rows. 71 (73: 73: 75: 77: 79) sts.
Dec 1 st at each end of next 3 rows, then
on foll alt row, then on 7 foll 4th rows.
49 (51: 51: 53: 55: 57) sts.
Work 1 row.
Dec 1 st at each end of next and every foll alt row
to 41 sts, then on foll 5 rows, ending with a WS row.
Cast off rem 31 sts.

MAKING UP

Press all pieces with a warm iron over
a damp cloth.
Join both shoulder seams using back stitch
or mattress stitch if preferred.

Neckband

With RS facing and using 2mm (US 0) needles,
starting and ending at back opening edges,
pick up and knit 24 (25: 25: 26: 26: 26) sts
from left back neck, 22 (22: 22: 25: 25: 25) sts
down left side of neck, 26 (28: 28: 28: 28: 28)
sts from front, 22 (22: 22: 25: 25: 25) sts up
right side of neck, then 24 (25: 25: 26: 26: 26)
sts from right back neck.
118 (122: 122: 130: 130: 130) sts.
Beg with row 2, work in rib as given for back
for 6 rows, ending with a **RS** row.
Cast off in rib (on **WS**).
Join side seams. Join sleeve seams. Insert
sleeves into armholes.
Using 2.50mm (US C2) crochet hook, attach yarn
at top of neckband and work a row of double
crochet around entire back opening edge, ending
at top of neckband and making 2 buttonloops
along right back end of neckband.
Fasten off.
Sew on buttons to correspond with buttonloops.

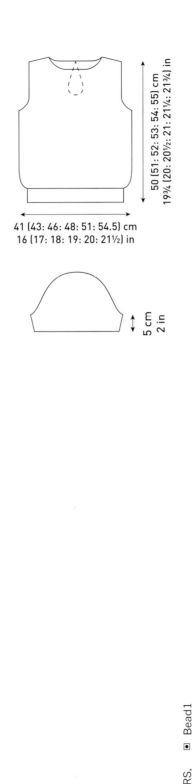

50 (51: 52: 53: 54: 55) cm
19¾ (20: 20½: 21: 21¼: 21¾) in

41 (43: 46: 48: 51: 54.5) cm
16 (17: 18: 19: 20: 21½) in

5 cm
2 in

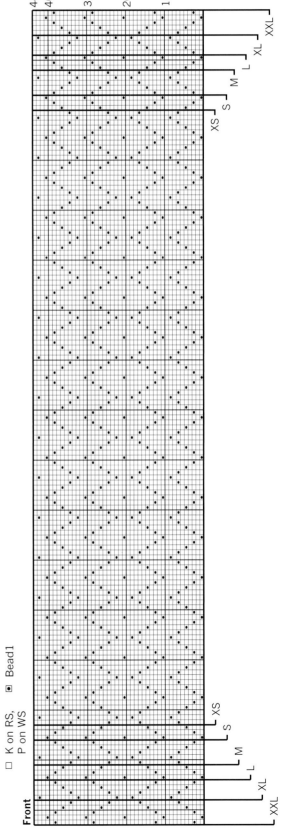

Key

☐ K on RS,
P on WS

⊡ Bead1

44 row patt rep

Front

LUSTRE
Neat cardigan with beading

Recommendation
Suitable for the knitter with a little experience
Please see pages 52, 53 & 55 for photographs.

	XS	S	M	L	XL	XXL	
To fit	**81**	**86**	**91**	**97**	**102**	**109**	cm
bust	32	34	36	38	40	43	in

Rowan Pima Cotton DK

    5   6   6   7   7   8 x 50gm
Photographed in Fig

Needles
1 pair 3mm (no 11) (US 2/3) needles
1 pair 3¼mm (no 10) (US 3) needles

Buttons – 8

Beads - approx 1210 (1310: 1400: 1540: 1670: 1830) size 8 beads

Tension
26 sts and 34 rows to 10 cm measured over pattern using 3¼mm (US 3) needles.

SPECIAL ABBREVIATIONS
BC2 = slide a bead up next to st just worked, yrn, P2, keeping bead at RS (back) of work now lift the "yrn" over last 2 P sts and off right needle, leaving bead sitting in front of these 2 P sts on RS of work. See page 98 for further details.

BACK
Cast on 94 (100: 106: 114: 120: 130) sts using 3mm (US 2/3) needles.
Row 1 (RS): K0 (1: 0: 0: 0: 0), P0 (2: 2: 2: 1: 2), *K2, P2, rep from * to last 2 (1: 0: 0: 3: 0) sts, K2 (1: 0: 0: 2: 0), P0 (0: 0: 0: 1: 0).
Row 2: P0 (1: 0: 0: 0: 0), K0 (2: 2: 2: 1: 2), *P2, K2, rep from * to last 2 (1: 0: 0: 3: 0) sts, P2 (1: 0: 0: 2: 0), K0 (0: 0: 0: 1: 0).
These 2 rows form rib.
Cont in rib until back measures 5 cm, ending with a WS row.
Change to 3¼mm (US 3) needles.
Beg with a K row, work in st st for 2 rows.
Next row (inc) (RS): K2, M1, K to last 2 sts, M1, K2. 96 (102: 108: 116: 122: 132) sts.
Working all increases as set by last row, now work in patt as folls:
Row 1 (WS): Purl.
Row 2 and every foll alt row: Knit.
Row 3: P5 (2: 5: 3: 6: 5), BC2, *P4, BC2, rep from * to last 5 (2: 5: 3: 6: 5) sts, P5 (2: 5: 3: 6: 5).
Row 5: Purl.
Row 7: P2 (5: 2: 6: 3: 2), BC2, *P4, BC2, rep from * to last 2 (5: 2: 6: 3: 2) sts, P2 (5: 2: 6: 3: 2).
Row 8: Knit.
These 8 rows form patt.
Cont in patt, inc 1 st at each end of 10th and foll 18th row, taking inc sts into patt.
100 (106: 112: 120: 126: 136) sts.
Cont straight until back measures 20 (20: 21: 21: 21: 21) cm, ending with a WS row.
Shape armholes
Keeping patt correct, cast off 4 (4: 5: 5: 6: 6) sts at beg of next 2 rows.
92 (98: 102: 110: 114: 124) sts.
Dec 1 st at each end of next 3 (3: 5: 5: 7: 7) rows, then on foll 1 (3: 2: 4: 3: 6) alt rows, then on foll 4th row. 82 (84: 86: 90: 92: 96) sts.
Cont straight until armhole measures 17 (18: 18: 19: 20: 21) cm, ending with a WS row.
Shape shoulders and back neck
Cast off 7 (7: 7: 8: 8: 9) sts at beg of next 2 rows. 68 (70: 72: 74: 76: 78) sts.
Next row (RS): Cast off 7 (7: 7: 8: 8: 9) sts, patt until there are 11 (11: 12: 11: 12: 12) sts on right needle and turn, leaving rem sts on a holder.

Work each side of neck separately.
Cast off 4 sts at beg of next row.
Cast off rem 7 (7: 8: 7: 8: 8) sts.
With RS facing, rejoin yarn to rem sts, cast off centre 32 (34: 34: 36: 36: 36) sts, patt to end. Complete to match first side, reversing shapings.

Pattern note: Row-end edges of fronts forms actual front opening edges. To ensure edges remains neat and tidy, make sure new balls of yarn are joined in at side seam edges **only**.

LEFT FRONT
Cast on 54 (57: 60: 64: 67: 72) sts using 3mm (US 2/3) needles.
Row 1 (RS): K0 (1: 0: 0: 0: 0), P0 (2: 2: 2: 1: 2), *K2, P2, rep from * to last 10 sts, K2, P1, K7.
Row 2: K8, *P2, K2, rep from * to last 2 (1: 0: 0: 3: 0) sts, P2 (1: 0: 0: 2: 0), K0 (0: 0: 0: 1: 0).
These 2 rows set the sts - front opening edge 8 sts in border patt and rem sts in rib.
Cont as set until left front measures 5 cm, ending with a WS row.
Change to 3¼mm (US 3) needles.
Next row (RS): K to last 8 sts, P1, K7.
Next row: K8, P to end.
Next row (inc): K2, M1, K to last 8 sts, P1, K7. 55 (58: 61: 65: 68: 73) sts.
Working all increases as set by last row, now work in patt as folls:
Row 1 (WS): K8, P to end.
Row 2 and every foll alt row: K to last 8 sts, P1, K7.
Row 3: K8, *P4, BC2, rep from * to last 5 (2: 5: 3: 6: 5) sts, P5 (2: 5: 3: 6: 5).
Row 5: K8, P to end.
Row 7: K8, P1, BC2, *P4, BC2, rep from * to last 2 (5: 2: 6: 3: 2) sts, P2 (5: 2: 6: 3: 2).
Row 8: As row 2.
These 8 rows set the sts - 8 st front opening edge border and all other sts in patt as given for back.
Cont as now set, inc 1 st at beg of 10th and foll 18th row, taking inc sts into patt.
57 (60: 63: 67: 70: 75) sts.
Cont straight until left front matches back to start of armhole shaping, ending with a WS row.

Shape armhole

Keeping patt correct, cast off 4 (4: 5: 5: 6: 6) sts at beg of next row.
53 (56: 58: 62: 64: 69) sts.
Work 1 row.
Dec 1 st at armhole edge of next 3 (3: 5: 5: 7: 7) rows, then on foll 1 (3: 2: 4: 3: 6) alt rows, then on foll 4th row.
48 (49: 50: 52: 53: 55) sts.
Cont straight until 18 (18: 18: 20: 20: 20) rows less have been worked than on back to start of shoulder shaping, ending with a WS row.

Shape front neck

Next row (RS): Patt 30 (30: 31: 33: 34: 36) sts and turn, leaving rem 18 (19: 19: 19: 19: 19) sts on a holder.
Keeping patt correct, dec 1 st at neck edge of next 6 rows, then on foll 2 (2: 2: 3: 3: 3) alt rows, then on foll 4th row.
21 (21: 22: 23: 24: 26) sts.
Work 3 rows, ending with a WS row.

Shape shoulder

Cast off 7 (7: 7: 8: 8: 9) sts at beg of next and foll alt row.
Work 1 row.
Cast off rem 7 (7: 8: 7: 8: 8) sts.
Mark positions for 8 buttons along left front opening edge - lowest button to come level with row 5, top button to come 1 cm above start of neck shaping, and rem 6 buttons evenly spaced between.

RIGHT FRONT

Cast on 54 (57: 60: 64: 67: 72) sts using 3mm (US 2/3) needles.
Row 1 (RS): K7, P1, *K2, P2, rep from * to last 2 (1: 0: 0: 3: 0) sts, K2 (1: 0: 0: 2: 0), P0 (0: 0: 0: 1: 0).
Row 2: P0 (1: 0: 0: 0: 0), K0 (2: 2: 2: 1: 2), *P2, K2, rep from * to last 10 sts, P2, K8.
These 2 rows set the sts - front opening edge 8 sts in border patt and rem sts in rib.
Cont as set for a further 2 rows, ending with a WS row.
Row 5 (buttonhole row) (RS): K3, K2tog tbl, yfwd (to make a buttonhole), patt to end.
Making a further 6 buttonholes in this way to correspond with positions marked for buttons on left front and noting that no further reference will be made to buttonholes, cont as folls:
Cont as set until right front measures 5 cm, ending with a WS row.
Change to 3¼mm (US 3) needles.
Next row (RS): K7, P1, K to end.
Next row: P to last 8 sts, K8.

Next row (inc): K7, P1, K to last 2 sts, M1, K2.
Working all increases as set by last row, now work in patt as folls:
Row 1 (WS): P to last 8 sts, K8.
55 (58: 61: 65: 68: 73) sts.
Row 2 and every foll alt row: K7, P1, K to end.
Row 3: P5 (2: 5: 3: 6: 5), BC2, *P4, BC2, rep from * to last 12 sts, P4, K8.
Row 5: P to last 8 sts, K8.
Row 7: P2 (5: 2: 6: 3: 2), BC2, *P4, BC2, rep from * to last 9 sts, P1, K8.
Row 8: As row 2.
These 8 rows set the sts - 8 st front opening edge border and all other sts in patt as given for back.
Complete as given for left front, reversing shapings and working first row of neck shaping as folls:

Shape front neck

Next row (RS): Patt 18 (19: 19: 19: 19: 19) sts and slip these sts onto a holder, patt to end.
30 (30: 31: 33: 34: 36) sts.

SLEEVES (both alike)

Cast on 70 (74: 74: 78: 82: 82) sts using 3mm (US 2/3) needles.
Row 1 (RS): K2, *P2, K2, rep from * to end.
Row 2: P2, *K2, P2, rep from * to end.
These 2 rows form rib.
Cont in rib until sleeve measures 3 cm, inc 1 (0: 1: 0: 0: 1) st at each end of last row and ending with a WS row.
72 (74: 76: 78: 82: 84) sts.
Change to 3¼mm (US 3) needles.
Now work in patt as folls:
Row 1 and every foll alt row: Knit.
Row 2 (WS): Purl.
Row 4: P5 (6: 7: 2: 4: 5), BC2, *P4, BC2, rep from * to last 5 (6: 7: 2: 4: 5) sts, P5 (6: 7: 2: 4: 5).
Row 6: Purl.
Row 8: P2 (3: 4: 5: 7: 2), BC2, *P4, BC2, rep from * to last 2 (3: 4: 5: 7: 2) sts, P2 (3: 4: 5: 7: 2).
These 8 rows form patt.
Work in patt for a further 2 rows, ending with a WS row.

Shape top

Keeping patt correct, cast off 4 (4: 5: 5: 6: 6) sts at beg of next 2 rows.
64 (66: 66: 68: 70: 72) sts.
Dec 1 st at each end of next 3 rows, then on foll alt row, then on 6 foll 4th rows.
44 (46: 46: 48: 50: 52) sts.
Work 1 row.
Dec 1 st at each end of next and every foll alt row to 40 sts, then on foll 7 rows, ending with a WS row.
Cast off rem 26 sts.

MAKING UP

Press all pieces with a warm iron over a damp cloth.
Join both shoulder seams using back stitch or mattress stitch if preferred.

Neckband

With RS facing and using 3mm (US 2/3) needles, slip 18 (19: 19: 19: 19: 19) sts on right front holder onto right needle, rejoin yarn and pick up and knit 21 (21: 21: 24: 24: 24) sts up right side of neck, 40 (42: 42: 44: 44: 44) sts from back, and 21 (21: 21: 24: 24: 24) sts down left side of neck, then patt 18 (19: 19: 19: 19: 19) sts on left front holder. 118 (122: 122: 130: 130: 130) sts.
Row 1 (WS): K8, P2, *K2, P2, rep from * to last 8 sts, K8.
Row 2: K3, K2tog tbl, yfwd (to make 8th buttonhole), K2, P1, K2, *K2, P2, rep from * to last 8 sts, P1, K7.
These 2 rows set the sts - 8 sts at each end of rows still in patt with all other sts in rib.
Cont as set for a further 4 rows, ending with a RS row.
Cast off in patt (on **WS**).
Join side seams. Join sleeve seams. Insert sleeves into armholes. Sew on buttons.

38 (40.5: 43: 45.5: 48: 52) cm
15 (16: 17: 18: 19: 20½) in

37 (38: 39: 40: 41: 42) cm
14½ (15: 15¼: 15¾: 16: 16½) in

6 cm
2 ½ in

INFORMATION
A guide to assist with techniques & finishing touches

TENSION

Achieving the correct tension has to be one of the most important elements in producing a beautiful, well fitting knitted garment. The tension controls the size and shape of your finished piece and any variation to either stitches or rows, however slight, will affect your work and change the fit completely.

To avoid any disappointment, we would always recommend that you knit a tension square in the yarn and stitch given in the pattern, working perhaps four or five more stitches and rows than those given in the tension note.

When counting the tension, place your knitting on a flat surface and mark out a 10cm square with pins. Count the stitches between the pins. If you have too many stitches to 10cm your knitting it too tight, try again using thicker needles, if you have too few stitches to 10cm your knitting is too loose, so try again using finer needles. Please note, if you are unable to achieve the correct stitches and rows required, the stitches are more crucial as many patterns are knitted to length.

Keep an eye on your tension during knitting, especially if you're going back to work which has been put to one side for any length of time.

SIZING

The instructions are given for the smallest size. Where they vary, work the figures in brackets for the larger sizes. One set of figures refers to all sizes. The size diagram with each pattern will help you decide which size to knit. The measurements given on the size diagram are the actual size your garment should be when completed.

Measurements will vary from design to design because the necessary ease allowances have been made in each pattern to give your garment the correct fit, i.e. a loose fitting garment will be several cm wider than a neat fitted one, a snug fitting garment may have no ease at all.

CHART NOTE

Some of our patterns include a chart. Each square on a chart represent a stitch and each line of squares a row of knitting.

When working from a chart, unless otherwise stated, read odd rows (RS) from right to left and even rows (WS) from left to right. The key alongside each chart indicates how each stitch is worked.

BEADING NOTE

Before starting to knit front and sleeves, thread beads onto yarn. To do this, thread a fine sewing needle (one that will easily pass through the beads) with sewing thread. Knot ends of thread and then pass end of yarn through this loop. Thread a bead onto sewing thread and then gently slide it along and onto knitting yarn. Continue in this way until required number of beads are on yarn. Do not place beads on edge sts of rows as this will interfere with seaming.
Beads can be purchased from
www.debbieabrahamsbeads.co.uk

FINISHING INSTRUCTIONS

It is the pressing and finishing which will transform your knitted pieces into a garment to be proud of.

Pressing

Darn in ends neatly along the selvage edge. Follow closely any special instructions given on the pattern or ball band and always take great care not to over press your work. Block out your knitting on a pressing or ironing board, easing into shape, and unless otherwise stated, press each piece using a warm iron over a damp cloth.

Tip: Attention should be given to ribs/edgings; if the garment is close fitting – steam the ribs gently so that the stitches fill out but stay elastic. Alternatively if the garment is to hang straight then steam out to the correct shape.

Tip: Take special care to press the selvages, as this will make sewing up both easier and neater.

CONSTRUCTION
Stitching together

When stitching the pieces together, remember to match areas of pattern very carefully where they meet. Use a stitch such as back stitch or mattress stitch for all main knitting seams and join all ribs and neckband with mattress stitch, unless otherwise stated.

Take extra care when stitching the edgings and collars around the back neck of a garment. They control the width of the back neck, and if too wide the garment will be ill fitting and drop off the shoulder.

Knit back neck edgings only to the length stated in the pattern, even stretching it slightly if for example, you are working in garter or horizontal rib stitch.

Stitch edgings/collars firmly into place using a back stitch seam, easing-in the back neck to fit the collar/edging rather than stretching the collar/edging to fit the back neck.

CARE INSTRUCTIONS
Yarns

Follow the care instructions printed on each individual ball band. Where different yarns are used in the same garment, follow the care instructions for the more delicate one.

Buttons

We recommend that buttons are removed if your garment is to be machine washed.

CROCHET

We are aware that crochet terminology varies from country to country. Please note we have used the English style in this publication.

Crochet abbreviations

ch	chain
ss	slip stitch
dc	double crochet
tr	treble
ttr	triple treble

Double crochet

1. Insert the hook into the work (as indicated in the pattern), wrap the yarn over the hook and draw the yarn through the work only.
2. Wrap the yarn again and draw the yarn through both loops on the hook.
3. 1 dc made

Treble

1. Wrap the yarn over the hook and insert the hook into the work (as indicated on the pattern).
2. Wrap the yarn over the hook draw through the work only and wrap the yarn again.
3. Draw through the first 2 loops only and wrap the yarn again.
4. Draw through the last 2 loops on the hook.
5. 1 treble made.

Triple Treble

1. Wrap the yarn over the hook 3 times and insert the hook into the work (as indicated on the pattern).
2. Wrap the yarn over the hook, draw through the work only and wrap the yarn again.
3. Draw through the first 2 loops only and wrap the yarn again.
4. Draw through the first 2 loops only and warp the yarn again.
5. Draw through the last 2 loops on the hook.
6. 1 treble made.

ABBREVIATIONS

K	knit
P	purl
K1b	knit 1 through back loop
st(s)	stitch(es)
inc	increas(e)(ing)
dec	decreas(e)(ing)
st st	stocking stitch (1 row K, 1 row P)
garter st	garter stitch (K every row)
beg	begin(ning)
foll	following
rem	remain(ing)
rev st st	reverse stocking stitch (1 row P, 1 row K)
rep	repeat
alt	alternate
cont	continue
patt	pattern
tog	together
mm	millimetres
cm	centimetres
in(s)	inch(es)
RS	right side
WS	wrong side
sl 1	slip one stitch
psso	pass slipped stitch over
tbl	through back of loop
M1	make one stitch by picking up horizontal loop before next stitch and knitting into back of it
M1p	make one stitch by picking up horizontal loop before next stitch and purling into back of it
yfwd	yarn forward (making a stitch)
yon	yarn over needle (making a stitch)
yrn	yarn round needle (making a stitch)-
MP	Make picot: Cast on 1 st, by inserting the right needle between the first and second stitch on left needle, take yarn round needle, bring loop through and place on left (one stitch cast on), cast off 1 st, by knitting first the loop and then the next stitch, pass the first stitch over the second (one stitch cast off).
Cn	cable needle
C4B	Cable 4 back: Slip next 2 sts onto a cn and hold at back of work, K2, K2 from cn.
C4F	Cable 4 front: Slip next 2 sts onto a cn and hold at front of work, K2, K2 from cn.

THANK YOU!

Firstly to our fantastic team;
Graham Watts, Diana Fisher, Fiona Beck,
Angela Lin, Sue Whiting, Tricia McKenzie,
Susan Laybourn, Ella Taylor, Sandra Richardson,
Betty Falconer, Glennis Garnet,
Margaret Oswald & Patricia Liddle.

Our grateful thanks also go to
Ann, Kate, David & the Rowan team
for their continuing support and
the lovely Rohanna for lending a hand
on the shoot.

Kim, Kathleen & Lindsay

INDEX